D0507597

Uniting
Academic and Behavior
Interventions

SOLVING THE SKILL OR WILL DILEMMA

Austin Buffum | Mike Mattos | Chris Weber | Tom Hierck

Solution Tree | Press

a division of
Solution Tree

Copyright © 2015 by Solution Tree Press

Materials appearing here are copyrighted. With one exception, all rights are reserved. Readers may reproduce only those pages marked "Reproducible." Otherwise, no part of this book may be reproduced or transmitted in any form or by any means (electronic, photocopying, recording, or otherwise) without prior written permission of the publisher.

555 North Morton Street
Bloomington, IN 47404
800.733.6786 (toll free) / 812.336.7700
FAX: 812.336.7790

email: info@solution-tree.com
solution-tree.com

Visit **go.solution-tree.com/rtiatwork** to download the reproducibles in this book.

Printed in the United States of America

18   17   5

Library of Congress Cataloging-in-Publication Data

Buffum, Austin G.
  Uniting academic and behavior interventions : solving the skill or will dilemma / Austin Buffum, Mike Mattos, Chris Weber, Tom Hierck.
    pages cm
  Includes bibliographical references and index.
  ISBN 978-1-936764-89-1 (perfect bound) 1. Remedial teaching. 2. Response to intervention (Learning disabled children) 3. Learning disabled children--Education. 4. Learning disabilities--Diagnosis. 5. Problem children--Behavior modification. I. Title.
  LB1029.R4B787 2015
  371.9--dc23
                              2014032296

Solution Tree
Jeffrey C. Jones, CEO
Edmund M. Ackerman, President

Solution Tree Press
President: Douglas M. Rife
Editorial Director: Lesley Bolton
Associate Acquisitions Editor: Kari Gillesse
Managing Production Editor: Caroline Weiss
Senior Production Editor: Suzanne Kraszewski
Proofreader: Jessi Finn
Cover and Text Designer: Laura Kagemann

I dedicate this book to my high school chemistry teacher, Mr. Richard Clark, who inspired me to become a teacher. Mr. Clark graduated from Caltech, and could do almost anything on that small slide rule he kept in his shirt pocket behind the plastic pocket protector. Special thanks go to Tim Stuart, Darrin Farney, and Dale Van Deven for their input on Anna.

—Austin Buffum

Growing up in 29 Palms, California, I was profoundly impacted by four teachers who strongly influenced my success in school and beyond: Ozzie Tsuneyoshi, Leo Flanagan, Jerry Foster, and Nolan Lockwood. I dedicate this book to these exceptional educators who continually remind me of the lifelong gifts a teacher can give a student.

—Mike Mattos

For teachers everywhere.

—Chris Weber

I have been fortunate to have excellent mentors during my career as an educator. Two, in particular, have shaped my thinking as it appears in this book, and I want to acknowledge their impact: Tom Johnson, the best coadministrator a person could hope for, who demonstrated daily a profound belief in the capacity of kids, and Wayne Hulley, who reminds us that parents send us the best kids they have, and we have a responsibility to be the best teachers those kids have.

—Tom Hierck

Acknowledgments

It seems inadequate that only our names are listed on the cover of this book; there are so many people who made this book possible. First and foremost, we would like to thank the outstanding professionals at Solution Tree. We believe Solution Tree, guided by the visionary leadership of Jeffrey C. Jones, is the preeminent educational publishing and professional development company in the world. We would like to specifically thank Solution Tree Press's president, Douglas M. Rife, for his patience and his advice to develop not a first draft, but a best draft of this book. We owe a debt of gratitude to the editor of this book, Sue Kraszewski, who did a masterful job of combining the work of four authors into one clear, cohesive voice. The staff development and institutes departments, led by Shannon Ritz and Kim Ennis, have been invaluable at making our work accessible to educators throughout the world, while Stubby McLean has expertly supported our work in Canada. Finally, Gretchen Knapp has been absolutely indispensable to our efforts, originally as the editor of our first three books, and now as the vice president of marketing. We hope this book moves Solution Tree one step closer to achieving its vision of transforming education worldwide.

The systematic behavior interventions included in this book are grounded squarely in the research of positive behavior interventions and supports (PBIS). These recommendations, developed by researchers including George Sugai and Rob Horner, have made a significant difference in how schools are supporting student behavioral needs. While we did not collaborate directly with these researchers on this book, we want to acknowledge and thank them for their collective contributions to our profession.

Finally, no one has had a greater impact on our work than the creators of Professional Learning Communities at Work™: Richard DuFour, Robert Eaker, and Rebecca DuFour. Their efforts continue to transform schools throughout the world and have had an immeasurable impact on our thinking. We are forever grateful for their generosity, their friendship, and their tireless efforts on behalf of students and educators.

Solution Tree Press would like to thank the following reviewers:

Calista Alden
Dean of Students
Westwood Intermediate School
Blaine, Minnesota

Shelby Jasmer
Director of RTI and Accountability
Cartwright School District
Phoenix, Arizona

Jeremy Koselak
Interventionist
Palmer High School
Colorado Springs, Colorado

Susan Leet
Continuous Improvement Coach
Westwood Intermediate School
Blaine, Minnesota

Bill Link
RTI/PBIS Coordinator
Vancouver Public Schools
Vancouver, Washington

Christine Zimmer
RTI Coordinator
Madison Elementary School
Madison, New Hampshire

Visit **go.solution-tree.com/rtiatwork**
to download the reproducibles in this book.

Table of Contents

About the Authors ix

The Chicken *and* the Egg 1

    The Life-Changing Impact of Success or Failure in School 2

    Higher Levels of Education and Training 2

    Lifelong Learning 3

    Individual Responsibility and Collaboration 4

    Implications for Educators 7

    Professional Learning Communities 7

    Response to Intervention 8

    Schoolwide Positive Behavior Supports 9

    Three Complementary Processes, One Outcome 10

    The Wrong Question 12

    Our Journey 14

1 Building the Foundation 17

    Not "All for One," but "All for All" 17

    The Four Cs of RTI at Work 21

2 The Five Students and Their Schools 29

    Armando and Robinson Elementary 30

    Katie and Wilson Elementary 32

    Holly and Roosevelt Elementary 35

    Franklin and Middletown Middle School 37

    Anna and Heartland High School 39

3 Protocols and Problem Solving 43

    The Pro-Solve Intervention Targeting Process 44

    Examining the RTI at Work Pyramid 46

    Applying the Pro-Solve Process to Tier 1 and Tier 2 49

    Putting the *R* in RTI 54

4 Uniting Core Instruction and Interventions **61**

Adopting Fundamental Assumptions. 61

Concentrating Instruction 62

Using Data 66

Armando and Robinson Elementary 69

Katie and Wilson Elementary 72

Holly and Roosevelt Elementary 73

Franklin and Middletown Middle School 74

Anna and Heartland High School 75

5 Uniting Skill and Will With Supplemental Interventions **77**

Targeting Interventions 77

Addressing Social and Academic Behaviors 80

Employing Behavioral Strategies. 82

Monitoring Progress. 82

Armando and Robinson Elementary 84

Katie and Wilson Elementary 89

Holly and Roosevelt Elementary 90

Franklin and Middletown Middle School 93

Anna and Heartland High School 97

6 Uniting Core Instruction and Intensive Remediation **107**

Two Critical Teams 109

Identifying Students for Intensive Interventions 112

Applying the Pro-Solve Process to Tier 3 116

Armando and Robinson Elementary 123

Katie and Wilson Elementary 125

Holly and Roosevelt Elementary 128

Franklin and Middletown Middle School 131

Anna and Heartland High School 134

Critical Considerations 138

Special Education Identification 144

7 Getting Started and Getting Better **147**

The Five Students and the Four Cs. 147

Taking Responsibility for All Learners 150

The Four Cs 150

References and Resources **155**

Index **159**

About the Authors

 **Austin Buffum, EdD,** has thirty-eight years of experience in public schools. His many roles include serving as former senior deputy superintendent of the Capistrano Unified School District in California. Austin has presented in over five hundred school districts throughout the United States and around the world. He delivers trainings and presentations on the RTI at Work™ model. This tiered approach to RTI is centered on Professional Learning Communities at Work™ (PLC) concepts and strategies to ensure every student receives the time and support necessary to succeed. Austin also delivers workshops and presentations that provide the tools educators need to build and sustain PLCs.

Austin was selected 2006 Curriculum and Instruction Administrator of the Year by the Association of California School Administrators. He attended the Principals' Center at the Harvard Graduate School of Education and was greatly inspired by its founder, Roland Barth, an early advocate of the collaborative culture that defines PLCs today. Austin later led Capistrano's K–12 instructional program on an increasingly collaborative path toward operating as a PLC. During this process, thirty-seven of the district's schools were designated California Distinguished Schools, and eleven received National Blue Ribbon recognition. Austin is coauthor of *Generations at School: Building an Age-Friendly Learning Community*.

A graduate of the University of Southern California, Austin earned a bachelor of music and received a master of education with honors. He also holds a doctor of education from Nova Southeastern University.

Mike Mattos is an internationally recognized author, presenter, and practitioner. Mike is an architect of the PLC at Work™ process, and is a cocreator of the RTI at Work™ model, which builds on the foundation of the professional learning community by using team structures and a focus on learning, collaboration, and results to successfully create multitiered systems of support.

Mike is former principal of Marjorie Veeh Elementary School and Pioneer Middle School in California. At both schools, Mike helped create powerful PLCs, improving learning for all students. In 2004, Marjorie Veeh, an elementary school with a large population of youth at risk, was named a California Distinguished School and won the Title I Academic Achievement Award.

A National Blue Ribbon School, Pioneer is among only thirteen schools in the United States selected by the GE Foundation as a Best-Practice Partner and is one of eight schools chosen by Richard DuFour to be featured in the video series *The Power of Professional Learning Communities at Work™: Bringing the Big Ideas to Life* (2007). Based on standardized test scores, Pioneer ranks among the top 1 percent of California secondary schools and, in 2009 and 2011, was named Orange County's top middle school. For his leadership, Mike was named the Orange County Middle School Administrator of the Year by the Association of California School Administrators.

To learn more about Mike Mattos and his work, visit http://mattos.info or follow him on Twitter @mikemattos65.

Chris Weber, EdD, is an expert in behavior, mathematics, and RTI who consults and presents internationally to audiences on important topics in education. As a principal and assistant superintendent in California and Chicago, Chris and his colleagues developed RTI systems that have led to high levels of learning at schools across the country.

In addition to writing and consulting, he continues to work with teachers and students every day as director of instruction for Distinctive Schools in Chicago and at some of the highest performing urban schools.

Chris has been in service to community and country his entire life. A graduate of the U.S. Air Force Academy, he flew C-141s during his military career. He is also a former high school, middle school, and elementary school teacher and administrator.

To learn more about Chris Weber and his work, visit www.chriswebereducation.com or follow him on Twitter @chi_educate.

Tom Hierck has been an educator since 1983 in a career that has spanned all grade levels and many roles in public education. His experiences as a teacher, administrator, district leader, Department of Education project leader, and executive director have provided a unique context for his education philosophy.

Tom is a compelling presenter, infusing his message of hope with strategies culled from the real world. He understands that educators face unprecedented challenges and knows which strategies will best serve learning communities. Tom has presented to schools and districts across North America with a message of celebration for educators seeking to make a difference in the lives of students. His dynamic presentations explore the importance of positive learning environments and the role of assessment to improve student learning. His belief that "every student is a success story waiting to be told" has led him to work with teachers and administrators to create positive school cultures and build effective relationships that facilitate learning for all students.

To learn more about Tom Hierck and his work, visit www.tomhierck.com or follow him on Twitter @thierck.

To book Austin, Mike, Chris, or Tom for professional development, contact pd@solution-tree.com.

The Chicken *and* the Egg

Which came first: the chicken or the egg? This question has been debated for centuries. Aristotle claimed the chicken must have come first "for there could not have been a first egg to give a beginning to birds, or there should have been a first bird which gave a beginning to eggs; for a bird comes from an egg" (Fénelon, 1825, p. 202). Charles Darwin argued the opposite, that the egg must have come first, assuming the question intended *egg* to mean an egg in general, rather than an egg that hatches into a chicken ("Chicken or the Egg," n.d.). The question remains equally provocative today, with some of our most respected scientific minds, like Stephen Hawking, offering insights into the debate. (If you're wondering, Hawking is an egg supporter [The Bridge School, 2005].)

Far from trivial, this question represents a much deeper discourse about the origins of life and how we view the universe. As Roman philosopher Macrobius stated:

> You jest about what you suppose to be a triviality, in asking whether the hen came first from an egg or the egg from a hen, but the point should be regarded as one of importance, one worthy of discussion, and careful discussion at that. (Smith & Daniel, 2000, p. 169)

Within the educational universe, we face our own chicken-or-egg dilemma regarding students who are at risk. We know that some students struggle in school for academic reasons—that is, they lack essential skills and knowledge needed to succeed in core curriculum. For other students, their struggles are due to an inability to consistently demonstrate the behaviors and motivation necessary for academic success. Our students most at risk usually demonstrate both problems, as there is a strong connection between low academic skills and problem behavior (Fleming, Harachi, Cortes, Abbott, & Catalano, 2004; Morrison, Anthony, Storino, & Dillon, 2001; Nelson, Benner, Lane, & Smith, 2004). To successfully intervene when students demonstrate academic and behavioral difficulties, we must answer our chicken-or-egg question: Is a student's behavior creating the academic struggles, or are the academic struggles prompting the negative behaviors?

Call it the skill-or-will dilemma. This vexing question is hardly a triviality and certainly demands careful discussion. Successful interventions require educators to address the cause of the student's difficulties, not just the symptoms, and focusing on the skill-or-will question forces us to pinpoint the origin of a particular student's struggles. Answer the question correctly, and educators can greatly increase a student's chances of succeeding in school and beyond, but answer the question incorrectly, and the consequences for the student can be catastrophic.

The Life-Changing Impact of Success or Failure in School

Just as answering the chicken-or-egg dilemma forces one to consider a larger view of the entire universe, so the skill-or-will dilemma requires educators to reflect on the very purpose of K–12 education. Peel back the layers of federal, state, provincial, and local requirements placed on schools today, and the fundamental purpose of our work is quite simple: schools are here to prepare children to be adults. As educators, it is our job to ensure our students learn the essential academic skills, knowledge, and dispositions needed to succeed in their adult life. Achieving this goal not only serves children, but also secures our collective future prosperity.

So if schools exist to prepare students to be adults, then we, as educators, must have an accurate vision of the future for which we are preparing our students. Undeniably, the world our students will compete in is not the world most current educators were preparing for when progressing through the K–12 system. Our world has changed radically and permanently, driven primarily by technological advances that are transforming how we work, communicate, think, and live. Let us consider the defining characteristics of this new world and what will be required of students hoping to succeed in it.

Higher Levels of Education and Training

To make a living above the rate of poverty, our students are going to have to continue to learn after high school. In 2012, about one-third of jobs were in occupations that typically require postsecondary education for entry (Bureau of Labor Statistics, 2013). By 2020, there will be fifty-five million new job openings in the United States. Twenty-three million will be for jobs that don't currently exist, and 65 percent of all jobs will require some level of postsecondary education and training (Gunderson,

2013). Occupations that typically require a master's degree for entry are projected to grow the fastest from 2012 to 2022, followed by associate's degree and doctoral or professional degree occupations (Bureau of Labor Statistics, 2013). And among traditional blue-collar trades, higher levels of academic preparation will be a prerequisite for employment. For example, the ACT (2006) examined math and reading skills required for electricians, construction workers, upholsterers, and plumbers and concluded they match what's necessary to do well in first-year college courses.

Additionally, wages for careers that require higher levels of education and training will outpace nondegreed jobs, with the average college graduate earning 77 percent more than the typical high school graduate (Bureau of Labor Statistics, 2013).

In 2011, males and females aged twenty-five to thirty-four with a bachelor's degree earned 69 and 70 percent more, respectively, than those without one (Weiner, 2013). According to Harvard University economists Claudia Goldin and Lawrence Katz (2007), from 1980 to 2005, the college wage premium—the amount of additional money earned by those with a college degree—increased by "an astonishing 25 percent." The rate of return for each year of college education now stands at about 13 to 14 percent (Goldin & Katz, 2007). This trend will continue a growing "education gap," in which access to a middle-class or better lifestyle will require post–high school learning (Mortenson, 2007).

As Craig D. Jerald (2009) states in *Defining a 21st Century Education*:

> The demand for educated workers will continue to be high, and those who obtain postsecondary education or training can continue to expect to earn a premium while those who do not will have far fewer opportunities to earn a living wage. (p. 30)

Lifelong Learning

In the 21st century workplace, our students will not have a job or a career, but jobs and careers. This means that earning a postsecondary degree or certificate does not mark the end of one's learning, but is merely a prerequisite to join a profession. According to the RAND study *The 21st Century at Work: Forces Shaping the Future Workforce and Workplace in the United States* (Karoly & Panis, 2004):

> Rapid technological change and increased international competition place the spotlight on the skills and preparation of the workforce, particularly the ability to adapt to changing technologies and shifting product demand. Shifts in the nature of business organizations and the growing importance of knowledge-based work also favor strong non-routine cognitive skills, such as abstract reasoning, problem solving, communication, and collaboration. Within this context, education and training become a continuous

> process throughout the life course involving training and retraining that continues well past initial entry into the labor market. . . . We can expect a shift away from more permanent, lifetime jobs toward less permanent, even nonstandard employment relationships (e.g., self-employment) and work arrangements (e.g., distance work). (p. xiv)

As James O'Toole and Edward Lawler (2006) state in *The New American Workplace*:

> The increasing speed of technology change, the increasing sophistication of foreign competitors, the export of manufacturing jobs, downsizing due to pressure to increase productivity amount to an almost perfect storm, creating an ever-increasing need for workers to update their skills regularly and, often, to develop entirely new ones. (p. 127)

For our students, learning must be a never-ending process.

Individual Responsibility and Collaboration

Due to an ever-increasing competitive global economy, successful businesses have moved from a costly, hierarchical leadership structure characterized by layers of management to a more "flattened" organizational structure in which employees work in teams that take a project from concept to completion. Due to this flattening out of the organizational structure, employees will be expected to take much greater responsibility for managing and taking responsibility for their work (Jerald, 2009).

Although employees will be required to take greater personal responsibility, this does not mean they will be working in isolation. Quite the contrary—the result of a flattened work structure is a greater reliance on project-based teams to achieve organization goals. And due to advances in technology and social media, the concept of a team is not limited to proximity or locale. As Thomas Friedman writes in his book *The World Is Flat* (2005), "Suddenly more people from more different places could collaborate with more other people on more different kinds of work and share more different kinds of knowledge than ever before" (p. 194).

If the new global economy is defined by jobs that require higher levels of prerequisite education and ongoing training and workers who have the ability to work independently and cooperatively, then what must all students learn during their K–12 education to be properly prepared for these demands? Certainly, our students will need to learn more than the three *R*s or merely possess the ability to score proficient on current high-stakes, standardized end-of-year assessments. Instead, every student must become a true lifelong learner, possessing the skills and knowledge needed to continue to learn beyond high school. Additionally, every student must master the behaviors necessary to be self-responsible and to collaborate effectively with others.

Specifically, we can categorize these outcomes into three types of essential learning: academic skills and knowledge, academic behaviors, and social behaviors.

Academic Skills and Knowledge

Academic skills and knowledge are composed of the foundational skills, content knowledge, and higher-level thinking skills students need to be able to apply what they have learned. *Foundational skills* include:

- Reading, including phonological awareness, phonics, fluency, vocabulary, and comprehension

- Mathematics, including rounding, ordering, and comparing numbers; time and money; adding, subtracting, multiplying, and dividing numbers; fractions and decimals; rates, ratios, and proportions; algebraic expressions and equations; measurement and geometry; and statistics and probability

- Writing, including ideas, organization, and conventions

- English language, including functionally based oral and written expression

These foundational skills are essential to a student's ability to gain essential content knowledge and continue learning.

Content knowledge includes relevant information, concepts, and background pertaining to the various domains of the arts and sciences. As Jerald (2009) states:

> Subject matter knowledge and basic skills are important building blocks for the broader competencies gaining value in the 21st century. . . . Being able to think critically about a topic or solve a problem in a particular domain demands sufficient background knowledge about it. And an important aspect of creativity is making connections across domains of knowledge—something that is impossible unless someone knows enough in different domains to make such a connection. (p. 31)

The term *higher-level thinking*, including analysis, synthesis, and evaluation, was made popular in education in the 1950s with the publication of Bloom's taxonomy of educational objectives (Bloom, Engelhart, Furst, Hill, & Kratwohl, 1956). It is essential that students master these critical-thinking skills to be able to apply what they have learned to future situations, problems, and environments, as well as to adapt and create new ideas and connections. Examples of advanced thinking skills that have high leverage for students include David Conley's (2007) standards for success.

1. Analytical reading and discussion

2. Persuasive writing

3. Drawing inferences and conclusions from texts

4. Analyzing conflicting source documents

5. Supporting arguments with evidence

6. Solving complex problems with no obvious answer (p. 2)

Together, these three types of learning represent the academic skills and knowledge every student will need to successfully continue to learn within the K–12 system and beyond. The new Common Core State Standards (CCSS) were specially designed to address many of these essential academic outcomes.

Academic Behaviors

In addition to academic skills and knowledge, there are academic behaviors critical to developing a successful learner. These behaviors include:

- Metacognition—Knowledge and beliefs about thinking

- Self-concept—A student's belief in his or her abilities

- Self-monitoring—The ability to plan and prepare for learning

- Motivation—The ability to initiate and maintain interest in tasks

- Strategy—Techniques for organization and memorization of knowledge

- Volition—The efforts and techniques needed to stay motivated and engaged in learning

Unfortunately, many schools view academic behaviors such as motivation and volition as things the student must already possess. However, these academic behaviors are no different from the foundational skills of reading or writing; they are not inherent gifts that people are born with but instead skills that can, and must, be taught.

Social Behaviors

Success in a school and work environment requires the ability to consistently demonstrate socially appropriate behaviors. These social behaviors include a student's ability to self-monitor:

- Responsible verbal and physical interactions with peers and adults

- Appropriate language

- Respect for property and materials

- Regular attendance

Any educator knows that success in school, and in life, is virtually impossible if a student cannot consistently demonstrate these social behaviors. Unfortunately, many schools consider teaching these skills primarily the responsibility of the parents or fall into the trap of perpetuating the practice of "teaching" behavior by exclusively applying negative consequences to students who misbehave. This approach is akin to teaching reading by having a school zero-tolerance policy on illiteracy and devising an increasingly negative set of consequences for students who lack the ability to read, all the while never actually teaching struggling readers how to read. Like academic behaviors, these social skills must be explicitly and systematically taught.

Implications for Educators

For students who can master these academic skills and behaviors, doors of opportunity will be available to them that lead to a productive, successful adult life. Conversely, students who fail in these basic school skills will be more likely to earn a wage that will leave them barely capable of securing the basics of life—food, shelter, and clothing. If our job as educators is to prepare children to be adults, then success in school is no longer optional; we must *ensure* that every student succeeds in school.

To achieve this daunting task, schools must systematically and effectively respond when students struggle—*systematic* meaning that every child who needs the help receives it, regardless of his or her assigned teacher, and *effective* meaning that interventions are tailored to meet the individual needs of each student. Because there is no way a single teacher can meet the individual needs of every student assigned to his or her class, a school staff must create collaborative processes to respond when students struggle. Because some students lack essential academic skills, a school must provide effective academic interventions; because some students lack the behaviors and motivation needed to succeed, a school must provide effective behavior interventions; and because our students most at risk will likely face both academic and behavioral challenges, we must solve the skill-or-will dilemma. Fortunately, educators have three research-based, complementary processes to ensure that every student succeeds: professional learning communities (PLCs), response to intervention (RTI), and schoolwide positive behavior supports (SWPBS).

Professional Learning Communities

Developed by Richard DuFour, Robert Eaker, and Rebecca DuFour, a PLC engages in an ongoing process in which educators work collectively to ensure high levels of learning for their students. Utilizing job-embedded collaboration time, educators work in high-performing teams focused on four critical questions.

1. What do we expect students to learn?
2. How do we know when they have learned it?

3. How will we respond when students don't learn?

4. How will we respond when students have learned?

Members of a PLC do not simply participate in weekly meetings to coordinate curriculum, plan assessments, and discuss students; collaborative teams in a PLC work in "recurring cycles of collective inquiry and action research to achieve better results for the students they serve" (DuFour, DuFour, Eaker, & Many, 2010, p. 11). In layman's terms, schools that function as a PLC are continually learning together about best practices, applying what they have learned to improve student achievement, and collecting evidence to determine if their efforts are working.

When implemented effectively, the PLC process creates the learning-focused school culture, collaborative structures, instructional focus, and ongoing assessment processes necessary to systematically respond when students don't learn. PLCs do not endorse or dictate a specific curriculum, assessment product, or intervention program, but instead create processes that empower site educators to make these critical decisions based on the specific learning needs of their students.

Response to Intervention

RTI is a systematic process of tiered support to ensure every student receives the additional time and support needed to learn at high levels. RTI's underlying premise is that schools should not delay providing help for struggling students until they fall far enough behind to qualify for special education, but instead should provide timely, targeted, systematic interventions to all students who demonstrate the need (Buffum, et al., 2012). Traditionally, the RTI process is represented in the shape of a pyramid (figure I.1).

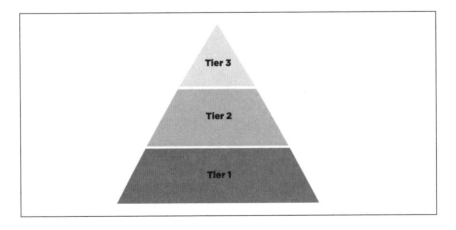

Figure I.1: The RTI pyramid.

The pyramid shape is wide at the bottom to represent the basic instruction that all students receive. As students demonstrate the need for additional support, they move up the pyramid, receiving increasingly more targeted and intensive help. Fewer students should need the services offered at the upper levels, thus creating the tapered shape of a pyramid. The pyramid is also traditionally separated into tiers, with Tier 1 representing grade-level core instruction, Tier 2 supplemental interventions, and Tier 3 intensive student support.

Like PLC, RTI does not endorse or dictate a specific curriculum, assessment product, or intervention program, but instead creates processes that empower educators to make these critical decisions based on the specific learning needs of their students. While RTI processes are applicable to behavior interventions, RTI implementation efforts have traditionally focused on academic curriculum and instructional practices (Sugai, 2001).

Schoolwide Positive Behavior Supports

Developed by George Sugai, Rob Horner, and their associates, SWPBS is a proactive, systematic approach for establishing the social culture and individualized behavior supports needed for schools to be effective learning environments for all students (Simonsen, Sugai, & Negron, 2008). Specifically, schools identify clear and measurable *outcomes* to improve student behavior and achievement; collect and use *data* to guide their decisions; implement relevant, evidence-based *practices*; and invest in *systems* that will ensure that practices are implemented with fidelity and sustained over time.

Like RTI, SWPBS is often represented in the shape of a pyramid (figure I.2).

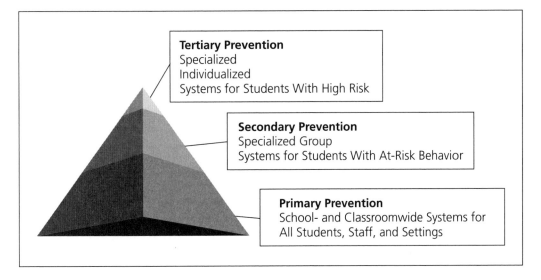

Source: Reprinted with permission from the OSEP Technical Assistance Center on Positive Behavioral Interventions & Supports (PBIS.org).

Figure I.2: PBIS pyramid for three tiers of schoolwide behavior support.

The base of the pyramid represents primary preventions—schoolwide efforts to teach and positively reinforce the academic and social behaviors needed to succeed in school. As students demonstrate at-risk behavior, support is tiered to provide targeted, supplemental help at the Tier 2 secondary level and highly individualized, intensive behavior interventions at the Tier 3 tertiary level.

Like PLC and RTI, SWPBS is not a program, but a process. It does not endorse or dictate a specific behavior curriculum, assessment product, or intervention program, but instead creates processes that empower site educators to make critical decisions based on the specific learning needs of their students.

Three Complementary Processes, One Outcome

PLC, RTI, and SWPBS are all processes focused on the same outcome—improved student learning. They are grounded in a common base of research, and many of the defining practices are identical (although they do not always use the same vocabulary). Where the processes are not the same, they are perfectly complementary. For example, PLCs focus on a learning-centered school culture and the collaborative structures necessary to achieve the goal of improved student learning. While PLCs address the need to collectively respond when students don't learn, they do not specifically describe the steps needed to create a system of interventions. Fortunately, RTI focuses specifically on how to create a tiered process of academic interventions, which would prove most helpful to schools functioning as a PLC in their efforts to answer the question, How will we respond when students don't learn? Yet RTI has not traditionally addressed exactly how to teach academic and social behaviors, or how to intervene when students need additional behavior support. Luckily, this is the focus of SWPBS. Finally, RTI and SWPBS require a learning-centered school culture and collaborative structures to be effective. While RTI and SWPBS do not specifically describe how to do this, PLCs do.

Despite the fact that PLCs, RTI, and SWPBS are research-based processes that have been endorsed by our profession's most respected researchers and organizations and implemented successfully at thousands of schools across North America, many schools continue to struggle to meet the needs of all their students, especially the ones most at risk. There are many reasons for this. Unfortunately, some schools defiantly refuse to take responsibility for student learning, instead opting to stick to the motto "It's our job to teach, and the kids' job to learn." Other schools continue to function like one-room schoolhouses, with individual teachers responsible only for "their" kids. Finally, some schools have tried to implement all three processes but view each as a separate program—they have all the pieces to a puzzle but can't see how they fit together.

Since the early 2000s, there have been targeted efforts to help schools connect the dots between PLCs, RTI, and SWPBS. In 2001, George Sugai introduced an integrated pyramid approach, combining academic interventions and behavior supports (figure I.3).

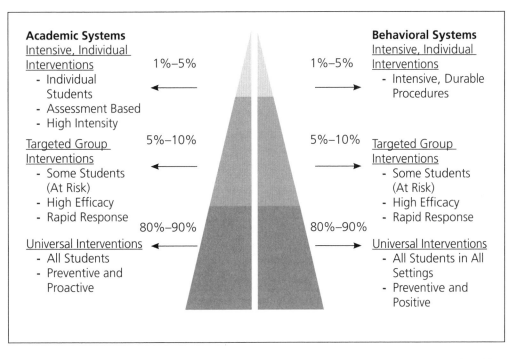

Source: Reprinted with permission from the OSEP Technical Assistance Center on Positive Behavioral Interventions & Supports (PBIS.org).

Figure I.3: Sugai's integrated split-pyramid approach combining academic and behavior interventions.

More recently, in our book *Pyramid Response to Intervention: RTI, Professional Learning Communities, and How to Respond When Kids Don't Learn* (Buffum, et al., 2009), we demonstrate how PLCs and RTI can be combined into a single process focused on learning. Likewise, our book *Pyramid of Behavior Interventions: Seven Keys to a Positive Learning Environment* (Hierck, Coleman, & Weber, 2011) combines PLCs and SWPBS into a singular, seamless process.

While these efforts helped clarify the connections and the importance of offering both academic and behavior interventions, they have still tended to reinforce a view that academic and behavior interventions are addressed by two separate programs. The interpretation is understandable, as even the integrated pyramid in figure I.3 visually divides the interventions into two distinct halves. When a school views academic and behavior interventions as two distinct parts of the pyramid, then determining the appropriate intervention for a particular student must begin with this question: Is the student's behavior creating his or her academic struggles, or are the academic struggles prompting the negative behavior? In other words, the question is whether it is a problem of skill or will, which brings us back to our chicken-or-egg dilemma.

The Wrong Question

The reason we struggle with the skill-or-will dilemma is because we are asking the wrong question. It is not a "chicken *or* egg" question, but rather a "chicken *and* egg" solution. If you were a farmer, and your goal was to successfully raise a flock of healthy chickens, you would not need chickens *or* eggs—you would need chickens *and* eggs. Likewise, if our job as educators is to raise healthy, productive, successful adults, our students will not need either the academic skills *or* the behaviors and dispositions needed to succeed as an adult, but both the skill *and* the will. In his book *Good to Great*, Jim Collins (2005) refers to this shift in thinking as the difference between the "tyranny of the OR" and the "genius of the AND." We believe that consistent and positive behavioral expectations and environments will lead to improved learning, *and* we believe that more engaging instruction will lead to improved behavior. Instead of creating processes and pyramids that separately address behavior and academics, we will consistently and avidly make the claim that they are interconnected and mutually reinforcing and thus must be viewed and implemented as a singular process.

In our book *Simplifying Response to Intervention: Four Essential Guiding Principles* (Buffum et al., 2012), we describe in very specific detail how a school or district can create such a process. Combining the foundational practices of PLCs, RTI, and SWPBS, we simplify the process into four essential principles, the four Cs.

1. **Collective responsibility**: A shared belief that the primary responsibility of each member of the organization is to ensure high levels of learning for every child. Thinking is guided by the question, Why are we here?

2. **Concentrated instruction**: A systematic process of identifying essential knowledge, skills, and behaviors that all students must master to learn at high levels, and determining the specific learning needs for each child to get there. Thinking is guided by the question, Where do we need to go?

3. **Convergent assessment**: An ongoing process of collectively analyzing targeted evidence to determine the specific learning needs of each child and the effectiveness of the instruction the child receives in meeting these needs. Thinking is guided by the question, Where are we now?

4. **Certain access**: A systematic process that guarantees every student will receive the time and support needed to learn at high levels. Thinking is guided by the question, How do we get every child there?

Consider for a moment the meaning of the word *essential*. When something is essential, it is absolutely indispensable—so important to the whole that the whole cannot survive without it. Without each of the four Cs, it is impossible for a school to achieve high levels of learning for every child. The four Cs work interdependently to create the systems, structures, and processes needed to provide every child with additional time and support.

Additionally, we provide a new visual to represent how a school should think about a schoolwide system of tiered student academic and behavior support: the RTI at Work™ pyramid, shown in figure I.4.

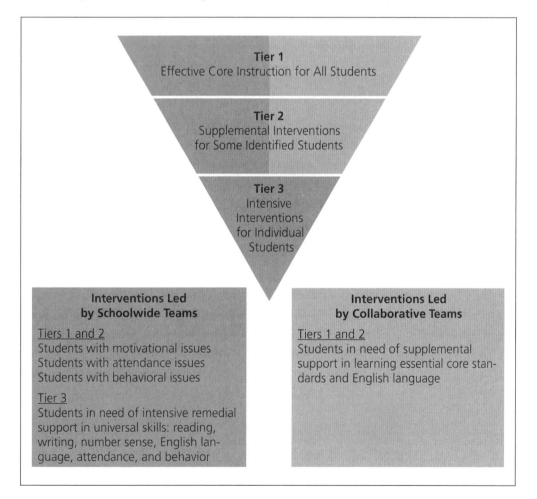

Figure I.4: The RTI at Work pyramid.

Utilizing collaborative teacher teams, a school leadership team, and a school intervention team, the RTI at Work pyramid is a visual representation of how a school can create both—taking collective responsibility for student learning and also delineating specifically who should take the lead responsibility for interventions relating to both skill (grade-level core content and foundational skills) and will (motivation, attendance, and behavior). We will describe the four *C*s and the RTI at Work pyramid in much greater detail in subsequent chapters.

Our purpose in writing *Simplifying Response to Intervention* (Buffum et al., 2012) was to provide an extremely clear vision of how the professionals within the building should work together to ensure all students learn. As such, the perspective of the book is focused on the work of the *adults* in the building. In this book, we want to follow the same process but change the vantage point: What would a unified system of academic and behavior supports look like for *individual students* who require help with both skill and will? In other words, what would academic and behavior interventions look like for students who face the skill-or-will dilemma?

Our Journey

In this book, we introduce you to five students: Armando, Katie, Holly, Franklin, and Anna.

While these students are fictitious, their attributes and needs are based on actual students we have served. These five students are designed to represent the spectrum of needs that are prevalent in schools across our nation, including:

- Different ages—Elementary, middle school, and high school aged
- Different demographics—Affluent and poor, English learners, and native English speakers
- Different settings—Large school and small school, rural and urban
- Different needs—Mild difficulties in skill and will to profound needs in both areas

Using the structure of the four *C*s and the RTI at Work pyramid, we will look specifically at potential academic and behavior supports for each student, as well as describe the collective processes the educators in the building would use to make these critical determinations. We then introduce an integrated "pro-solve" process to successfully determine, target, and monitor academic and behavior interventions, and we look at how schools can provide skill-and-will supports to each student within Tier 1 core instruction. We then discuss how schools can use Tier 2 supplemental interventions to support each student. Next, we demonstrate how to use Tier 3 intensive interventions when students have severe needs in academics and behavior. In the final chapter of the book, we identify ways in which schools can get started on this critical work. We will also suggest the steps that schools can take to continuously improve.

By the end of the book, our hope is that we, as educators, come to see students needing academic and behavior interventions not as a "dilemma," but instead as an opportunity for discovery. In place of our traditional reactive intervention practices that focus more on labeling struggling students as either skill *or* will problems, schools can create a tiered, proactive process that sees the whole child—the chicken *and* the egg—and can collectively and seamlessly provide whatever support each student needs to learn at high levels.

CHAPTER 1

Building the Foundation

One definition of *framework* is "the structure designed to support something." In this chapter, we outline the structures necessary to support the high levels of learning for all students that will prepare them for successful lives as adults. However, as sociologist Karen Hays (1994) points out, "[Structure] cannot easily be separated from the culture with which it is intertwined" (p. 67). The structures described in this chapter should not be seen as existing in isolation from the culture that surrounds them. Instead, as Richard Elmore (1996) suggests, it is ultimately the culture that creates lasting change at the "core of educational practice"—the classroom (p. 2).

We also believe that the following statement is true: when everyone is responsible, no one is responsible. When applied to schools and their implementation of RTI, we have often found that a schoolwide system of interventions has led general education teachers to believe they are responsible only for Tier 1 instruction. This often leads the classroom teachers to ask, "Who do I send them to when they don't learn in my class?" Conversely, and perhaps in response to this question, many districts become very directive in requiring that teachers cannot refer a student for schoolwide interventions until they have "proven" what they have first done in the classroom. To best meet the needs of every child, we should not pit one group of educators against another in this way. Rather than ask who should be responsible when students struggle—the classroom teacher *or* the schoolwide intervention system—we suggest that schools become crystal clear on who has the *lead* responsibility for certain groups of students or individual students.

Not "All for One," but "All for All"

One team takes the lead, but we all share responsibility for all students. This is a perfect example of how structure and culture interact. While it is important to help clarify who is responsible for what relative to RTI, ambiguity should be the enemy, not one another. Once we have clarified roles (structure), we remain committed to the idea that together, we are all responsible for the success of all students (culture). Accordingly, we believe that schools should clarify the roles of the following three teams: collaborative teacher teams, a schoolwide leadership team, and a schoolwide intervention team.

Collaborative Teacher Teams

Collaborative teacher teams are teams of educators who share essential student learning outcomes; these teachers of a common grade level or common course offering have worked together to determine what every student must master within their content. Once they have determined what these essential learnings are, they work together to ensure that every student receives the time and support necessary to be successful in attaining them.

By *team*, we do not mean loosely connected groups that assemble for traditional grade-level or department meetings. The act of meeting together does not define a group of people as a team. Typically, groups of educators meet together around some common topic or concern and then go back to their own classrooms and work in isolation, having very little impact on each other's efforts.

Members of a true team "work *interdependently* to achieve *common goals* for which members are mutually accountable" (DuFour et al., 2010, p. 3, emphasis in original). The common goals in this instance are the essential learning outcomes for all students, for which all team members take collective responsibility. These learning outcomes must include, in addition to academic, the social and behavioral "standards" the school and team have established as essential to the success of all students. Simply put, the collaborative teacher teams are responsible for seeing that all students know, understand, learn, and master these academic, social, and behavioral outcomes.

Of course, schoolwide resources must be made available to collaborative teams so that they might provide the core instruction and additional time and support to help every student be successful in the attainment of the standards. In fact, that is precisely the job of the next team we discuss: the schoolwide leadership team. However, we are suggesting that the collaborative teacher teams take the *lead* in designing the Tier 1 core instruction and implementing the school's response when students require additional instruction or intervention to achieve these critical learning outcomes.

The Schoolwide Leadership Team

Composed of representatives from each of the school's collaborative teacher teams, the schoolwide leadership team also includes administrative, classified, and support staff. The primary purpose of this team is to "unite and coordinate the school's collective efforts across grade levels, departments, and subjects" (Buffum et al., 2012, p. 36). To do this, the school leadership team takes the lead in creating a school culture in which collective responsibility for student achievement is the overarching principle driving the school, rather than the individual efforts of independent contractors who all respond differently when students struggle.

In addition to this important role of promoting cultural change, the school leadership team takes the lead in coordinating all of the human, fiscal, and time resources available to best support core instruction and interventions. For example, the scheduling of the school counselor, psychologist, speech and language pathologist, special education teachers, librarian, health services, subject specialists, instructional aides, and other classified staff is done by the school leadership team in such a way as to best support the work of the collaborative teacher teams. The school leadership team is also responsible for the creation of a master schedule that provides additional time and support for students as well as sufficient time for collaborative teacher teams to complete their important work.

The school leadership team should take the lead in clarifying schoolwide behavioral expectations and attendance policies. This is especially important in terms of our earlier discussion of the chicken and the egg. It makes sense for collaborative teacher teams to take the lead with essential academic outcomes; after all, they are credentialed in this area of the curriculum, they know the content the best, they have the assessment data, and they know the students the best. Similarly, it makes sense for a team, whose membership includes the school administration, counselor, psychologist, and special education teachers, to take the lead in defining the social and behavioral standards all students are to learn and exhibit. While the school leadership team takes the lead in this effort, in part because of its specialized experience and training, the collaborative teacher teams do not eschew all responsibility for these social and behavioral standards. Instead, they accept collective responsibility for helping all of their students understand and master these important standards, but the school leadership team takes the lead in defining and monitoring them.

Additionally, this team should take the lead in organizing the school's universal screening efforts for identifying those students desperately and immediately in need of Tier 3 support. Once again, while collaborative teacher teams participate in this screening effort, it is the school leadership team that accepts primary responsibility for selecting and organizing the administration of the school's universal screening tools.

Because the tasks of the school leadership team are so vital to the overall success of the school, and so connected to school culture, it is important that the team lead by example, not by fiat. School leadership teams "should unite the school's staff toward their mission of collective responsibility and coordinate the school's limited resources to best achieve this goal" (Buffum et al., 2012, p. 37). To do so, they must be very intentional in meeting frequently, not canceling meetings for "more urgent concerns," and set a calendar of dates from the beginning of the school year.

The Schoolwide Intervention Team

The schoolwide intervention team takes a detailed and diagnostic look at the cases of individual students who are in need of intensive Tier 3 support. Unlike the global, schoolwide focus of the leadership team, the intervention team applies laser-like focus to answering the question, What, specifically, are the causes of this individual student's struggles, and how can we provide him or her with additional time and support to address the causal factors? Students in need of intensive support most often struggle due to significant weaknesses in the foundational skills of reading, writing, number sense, and English language mastery; chronic and excessive absenteeism; severe behavioral or social concerns; and, most of the time, combinations of some or all of these factors.

Because of the severe nature of the concerns about many students in need of Tier 3 support, it is highly unlikely that an individual teacher, or even a team of teachers, would have the diverse expertise and all of the resources needed to provide the support that these students need. The school intervention team draws on the expertise of staff, including but not limited to the principal, counselor, psychologist, speech and language pathologist, nurse, special education teacher, English language development specialist, reading specialist, librarian, and community resource officer. In recognition of the fact that many schools may not have access to all of these resources on a regular basis, we encourage the kind of thinking that would identify the person on the staff best able to assume the role, even if he or she does not have the specific title. For instance, a school may not have a full- or part-time reading specialist, but may have a classroom teacher who has been highly trained and credentialed in the area of reading instruction or intervention.

The school intervention team should also meet frequently and regularly—not just in reaction to emergencies—to proactively offer timely solutions. A calendar of meeting dates should be established at the beginning of the year, and this meeting time must not be sacrificed to other demands.

We must apply new thinking to understanding the core purpose of the school intervention team. Unlike many school study teams (SSTs) of the past, the school intervention team's primary focus is on providing every possible resource to help students become successful, rather than rubber-stamping testing for special education placement. To streamline this process, schools may want to repurpose an existing SST. In doing so, schools must take great care to ensure that team members understand the proactive, problem-solving stance of the school intervention team.

The Four Cs of RTI at Work

Buffum et al. (2012), in *Simplifying Response to Intervention: Four Essential Guiding Principles*, articulate an alternative way of understanding and operationalizing RTI. The first essential guiding principle is collective responsibility, representing the fundamental purpose and moral imperative of our work as educators.

Collective Responsibility

The first *C, collective responsibility*, is "a shared belief that the primary responsibility of each member of the organization is to ensure high levels of learning for every child. Thinking is guided by the question: Why are we here?" (Buffum et al., 2012, p. 9). RTI is fundamentally and foundationally a framework for providing every student with the additional time and support needed to learn at high levels. To successfully employ instruction and interventions, all school staff must exhibit a continuous commitment within a culture of collective responsibility. A culture of collective responsibility is guided by a shared belief that the primary responsibility of every member of the organization is to ensure high levels of learning for every student. The PLC term for this tenet is a *focus on learning*: "educators within the organization embrace high levels of learning for all students as both the reason the organization exists and the fundamental responsibility of those who work within it" (DuFour et al., 2010, p. 11). Collective responsibility rests on this notion—we believe *all* students can learn at high levels and that *all* staff members are willing to do whatever it takes to ensure that this occurs. Collective responsibility defines a school's purpose and guides its actions.

Another PLC term that supports collective responsibility is *collaborative culture*, which is nurtured through "a *systematic* process in which [teachers] work together, interdependently, to analyze and *impact* their professional practice in order to improve individual and collective results" (DuFour et al., 2010, p. 120). Milbrey McLaughlin and Joan Talbert (2006) and others (DuFour et al., 2010; Hattie, 2009; Senge, 1990) have researched and written on the power of learning communities.

The notion of collective responsibility is neither new nor restricted to education. Peter Senge (1990) wrote a groundbreaking and prescient book *The Fifth Discipline*. The five disciplines are:

1. Personal mastery—Continually clarifying and deepening our personal vision, focusing our energies, developing patience, and seeing reality, objectively

2. Mental models—Challenging deeply ingrained assumptions, generalizations, or pictures of images that influence how we understand the world and how we take action

3. Building shared vision—Nurturing and unearthing shared pictures of the future that foster genuine commitment and enrollment rather than compliance

4. Team learning—Building the capacity of members of a team to suspend assumptions and enter into genuine thinking together

5. Systems thinking—Recognizing that a collective responsibility for the organization's mission is essential, and acting to ensure this responsibility is a reality

Every school's mission must be grounded in this belief: *all* staff will ensure high levels of learning for *all* students, whatever it takes. One would hope and think that every school and educator has assumed collective responsibility for the learning of all students; after all, virtually every school has a mission statement that references lifelong learning, high achievement, and 21st century skills. Sadly, mission statements, at times, have little meaning or impact on the beliefs and actions of educators. In too many schools, mission statements and actual practices represent opposing points of view. The discontinuity between idealized and actual school cultures, between learning for some and learning for all, between selective responsibility and collective responsibility, may be the most significant obstacle to schools' successful implementation of RTI.

To be clear, we believe that all educators must accept responsibility for the high levels of learning of every student. Parental, societal, and economic factors undoubtedly impact student learning, but the actions of educators can ultimately guarantee each student's success. We similarly believe that every student is capable of learning at high levels. We define high levels of learning as high school plus, meaning every student will graduate from high school ready for college or a skilled career and with the skills and knowledge required to continue to learn. A simple high school diploma is a ticket to nowhere (Waller, 1998). For RTI to be successful, a school's culture must passionately accept responsibility for every student and passionately believe in every student's unbounded capacity.

You will not find collaborative practices or the precepts of PLC in federal or state RTI guidelines. Unless RTI is implemented collectively and collaboratively, there is no way we can ensure that students will meet our high expectations. This cannot occur until all team members are able to answer "yes" to these two questions.

1. Do we truly believe that all students can learn at high levels?

2. Are we willing to do whatever it takes to ensure that this happens?

Concentrated Instruction

The second *C* is *concentrated instruction*: "A systematic process of identifying essential knowledge and skills that all students must master to learn at high levels, and determining the specific learning needs for each child to get there. Thinking is guided by the question: Where do we need to go?" (Buffum et al., 2012, p. 10). The foundation of building a system of supports that meets *all* the needs of *all* students is an intensive sense of collective responsibility, a commitment to working collaboratively, cooperatively, positively, and tirelessly on behalf of every student. The next step is to clearly identify, define, and communicate the content all students must learn. Let's frame concentrated instruction in terms of academic and behavioral standards. Have we identified and communicated the learning standards for each content area? Have we further identified the essential (or key, critical, or power) standards? Whether academic or behavioral, we have long known that there are too many standards for teachers to teach to mastery and for students to learn to the depth that is necessary (Mullis et al., 2007; Scherer, 2001).

However, concentrated instruction does not end with the identification of essential standards. Teachers and students must also understand what it looks and sounds like when students demonstrate mastery of the standards. In the verbiage of the day, the standards must be *unpacked*. Next, teachers must collaboratively scope and sequence standards (in a flexible curriculum map or pacing guide) so that the grade-level and content-area standards represent a guaranteed and viable curriculum (Marzano, 2003). Finally, teachers must explicitly, clearly, and consistently model mastery of these standards, both academic and behavioral. When teachers collaboratively identify essential standards, when they collaboratively unpack the standards, when the standards are scoped and sequenced into a guaranteed and viable curriculum, and when expectations are explicitly, clearly, and consistently modeled, then instruction has been concentrated.

This concept is certainly not new. Consider the first question of a PLC: "What is it we expect students to learn?" (DuFour et al., 2010). Robert Marzano describes this notion as a guaranteed, viable curriculum, by which every student has access to the same essential learning targets, regardless of teacher (guaranteed), that can be mastered in the allotted time (viable) (Marzano, 2003). Douglas Reeves (2002) describes the critical importance of concentrated instruction in *Making Standards Work*, Larry Ainsworth (2003a, 2003b) details these efforts in *Power Standards* and *"Unwrapping" the Standards*, and Grant Wiggins and Jay McTighe (2005) powerfully and comprehensively outline the essential work of concentrated instruction in *Understanding by Design*. Back in 1968, Benjamin Bloom (1968) proposed that *mastery learning* is a simple and powerful way of focusing and organizing our instructional efforts.

Concentrated instruction is neither a new nor a fly-by-night notion; it's essential, it's validated, and it has stood the test of time.

Our recent experiences suggest that this process has begun in academic domains, typically beginning with reading and mathematics, although the unpacking and explicit instruction components are less often completed. However, it is not as common for schools to complete the process fully for the social and academic behaviors that we expect of all students. If we do not clearly define, communicate, and model our expectations, we should not be surprised, or disappointed, if students do not meet them. The process of concentrating instruction can also facilitate the creation of common formative assessments and begins the process of convergent assessment.

Whether state, provincial, or CCSS, most would agree there are too many standards. If mastery, depth and complexity, problem solving, critical thinking, and engagement with 21st century skills for every student are the goals, and they *must* be, we must focus our standards. This will involve teams of teachers identifying those standards that are most essential, using protocols such as those Reeves (2002) and Ainsworth (2003a, 2003b) suggest, to reach consensus on the "must knows" and "nice to knows." These essential learnings, often referred to as *power standards*, must then be scoped and sequenced to build a guaranteed and viable curriculum. But this is not enough. There must also be consensus on the rigor and format of the essentials—what will it look like when students demonstrate mastery, and what types of tasks will students successfully complete? We must arrive at a consistent definition for mastery so that we can backwards plan and ensure that our differentiated instruction, and the differentiated tasks that we assign, will scaffold all students to high levels of learning.

Concentrated instruction, as implied in this section, is an ongoing process, not a one-time event. If teachers are to feel a sense of ownership in identifying what is essential for all students to learn, they must be involved in the determination of what is essential, not just handed a list created by others.

Convergent Assessment

The third *C* is *convergent assessment*: "An ongoing process of collectively analyzing targeted evidence to determine the specific learning needs of each child and the effectiveness of the instruction the child receives in meeting these needs. Thinking is guided by the question: Where are we now?" (Buffum et al., 2012, p. 10). Monitoring our instructional and intervention efforts is the engine that informs, motivates, and drives our systems of support for students. Once a school has created a collaborative culture focused on collective responsibility for student learning and has identified the learning goals all students must reach to be successful in school and in life, it should next gather the evidence necessary to determine each child's current levels of performance relative to the goals. *Response to intervention* is not simply a powerful lever for ensuring high levels of learning because of high-quality *instruction* and *intervention*; response to intervention is a powerful lever because educators frequently determine whether students are *responding* to core instruction and supplemental supports and, if students are not responding, make timely adjustments. Moreover, supports are effective when they are optimally targeted; assessments ensure that diagnoses inform instruction and interventions. Leading educators have validated the critical, central role that formative assessment and data-informed practices have in improved student learning and behavior. Larry Ainsworth and Donald Viegut (2006) detail the construction and use of convergent data in *Common Formative Assessments*. Dylan Wiliam (2011) describes how tests and data can be employed to converge our knowledge of student needs in *Embedded Formative Assessment*. Damian Cooper (2011) provides clarity on how assessment can, and must, be used when differentiating our practices in *Redefining Fair*. For decades, Thomas Guskey and Rick Stiggins have stressed that converging our knowledge of student needs using assessment is the central lever that transforms schools and student learning (Guskey, 2003; Stiggins, 2004). A paradox may exist in your schools—you feel that you administer too many assessments, yet you lack the information you need to adequately inform teaching and learning. We must leverage convergent assessment, a proven and widely accepted concept, in the analysis and use of data to continuously, and more diagnostically, inform our efforts on behalf of high levels of learning for every student.

Our assessments of all students, but particularly students at risk, must primarily be *formative*. In other words, they must inform our curricular and instructional decisions, allowing us to converge on the antecedents of student difficulties. Thus, our universal screening tools, diagnostic assessments, teacher-generated tests, and progress-monitoring probes must increasingly specify the supports that will benefit students. Cursory glances at the average percent correct on chapter tests are insufficient. We must analyze data on a by-the-student, by-the-standard, by-the-item basis. We must sit with individual students and "listen" to their thinking processes. We must consider all contributors to student difficulties, whether they are academic, behavioral, motivational, attentional, or from some other source.

Certain Access

The fourth *C* is *certain access*: "A systematic process that guarantees every student will receive the time and support needed to learn at high levels. Thinking is guided by the question: How do we get every child there?" (Buffum et al., 2012, p. 10). Even if educators passionately and collectively accept responsibility for all students; even if they focus, understand, and concentrate instruction; and even if they utilize assessments to screen, diagnose, monitor, and inform, if supports are not *systematically* implemented, RTI will be meaningless. RTI must ensure that every student receives the time and support needed to learn at the very highest levels and graduate high school ready for college or a skilled career. Lynn and Douglas Fuchs (2007), as well as Jack Fletcher and Sharon Vaughn (2009), have validated and described systems of support informed by RTI frameworks. The work of George Sugai and Robert Horner (2002) in the area of positive behavior interventions and supports (PBIS) and behavioral RTI has been transformative and terrifically impactful. William Bender (2009, 2012) has written extensively on RTI and the precepts of *Universal Design for Learning* (Dolan & Hall, 2001) are highly compatible with certain access and RTI. Finally, we have proudly described our work in schools in support of high levels of outcomes for all students using the principles of RTI in our previous books (Buffum et al., 2009, 2010, 2012; Hierck et al., 2011). RTI and certain access are validated and proven constructs.

Even when we have the *collective* will, the *concentrated* content, and the *convergent* information, if we do not alter the system, we will not make *certain* that all students have *access* to the time and supports they need to learn at high levels. Learning must be the constant. Time and support must be the flexible variables. Traditionally, in most schools, time and support have been constant, while learning has been variable. RTI requires that schools build, maintain, and revise systems of support that take into consideration:

- What—What materials, resources, and strategies are required to help educators meet the needs of students?

- Who—Which educator on campus, whether general or special educator, is best qualified and readily available to support students?

- When—When during the busy instructional day can students receive the supports that are essential to their success in school and in life?

Answering these questions is not simple, but they must be answered. Answering questions such as these ensures that schools have systems of support that guarantee access for all students to the time and supports that they need to learn at high levels.

The four *C*s are arguably the most researched way in which we can organize our efforts on behalf of all students. Consider the seminal, exhaustive studies conducted by John Hattie (2009). At the conclusion of his work *Visible Learning*, Hattie synthesized hundreds of educational research studies over several decades and concluded that the most powerful strategy for improving student learning occurs when teachers work together in collaborative teams to collectively complete the following tasks:

- Clarify what students must learn.

- Gather evidence of student learning.

- Analyze evidence of student learning.

- Identify the most effective teaching strategies.

Do these characteristics of the reflective, collaborative work of teams of teachers sound familiar? They are represented by the four Cs and will be applied throughout this book to describe how we can meet the needs of students who are experiencing difficulties with academic skills, social behaviors, and academic behaviors.

CHAPTER 2

The Five Students and Their Schools

In the introduction and chapter 1, we articulated our vision of RTI: a moral imperative and a (perhaps *the*) research-based way of ensuring that all students receive the time and supports they need to learn at high levels. In this chapter, we introduce you to five students with diverse academic, behavioral, and social challenges: Armando is a first-grade student with significant academic deficits and emerging noncompliant struggles. Katie is a fourth grader with worrying social-emotional needs and moderate reading gaps. Holly is a sixth-grade student with severe autism. Franklin is an eighth-grade student with very low levels of engagement and motivation who shows distracting behaviors. Anna is a tenth-grade student with significant needs in both academic and behavioral domains. The tiered supports that they receive from their teachers, as well as the types of school they attend, are shown in table 2.1.

Table 2.1: Student Characteristics

| Student Name | Grade Level | Tiers of Support (1, 2, or 3) Student Is Receiving | | | School Type |
		With Academics	With Social Behaviors	With Academic Behaviors	
Armando	1	1, 2, and 3	1 and 2	1	Small rural
Katie	4	1 and 2	1	1, 2, and 3	Larger
Holly	6	1, 2, and 3 with modified curriculum	1, 2, and 3 with modified curriculum	1, 2, and 3 with modified curriculum	Urban
Franklin	8	1	1, 2, and 3	1 and 2	Rural
Anna	10	1, 2, and 3	1, 2, and 3	1, 2, and 3	Suburban

In the remaining chapters of the book, we will apply the four *C*s to each of these students through the contexts of the types of Tier 1, Tier 2, and Tier 3 supports their schools provide. First, let's meet the students.

Armando and Robinson Elementary

Armando is a first-grade student at Robinson Elementary, a small K–8 school of 144 students in a rural farming community. Armando's parents do not speak English with confidence, and they rarely speak English with Armando. His three older siblings speak English well. Armando enjoys school and playing soccer. There are twenty students in Armando's class, and his teacher, Ms. Hollings, is the only first-grade teacher at the school. The school's single kindergarten and second-grade teachers comprise Ms. Hollings's collaborative teacher team. They collectively assume responsibility for the K–2 students at the school, supporting one another in the identification of essential standards, as well as unpacking and unwrapping essentials so that the teachers and students clearly understand the rigor and format required for mastery. The team also supports one another with the creation of common assessments, the analysis of data, and the design and delivery of Tier 2 supports.

There are ten classroom teachers at Robinson; the relatively large number of students in fourth and fifth grades requires three teachers. There is one fourth-grade classroom, one fifth-grade classroom, and one split class. There is a special education teacher and assistant to support students. A psychologist, counselor, and speech and language pathologist are on campus one day per week. The school repurposed teaching assistant positions years ago, and now a team of three interventionists works with collaborative teacher teams and schoolwide teams to provide tiered supports within a well-defined, systematic schedule.

Over the past three years, staff have participated in high-quality professional development on effective phonics instruction, developmental spelling, scaffolds for English learners, the use of graphic organizers across content areas, and the writing process. Robinson is located in a farming region, and the nearest school is nearly one hour away. Accordingly, staff collaborate bimonthly with colleagues remotely via Google+ Hangouts and grade-level and content-specific boards on Pinterest and other social media outlets.

There are challenges associated with a small school with a single teacher at each grade level; however, the vertical articulation achieved and the opportunities for cross-grade supports enhance both teaching and learning. Collaborative teacher teams, composed of K–2, 3–5, and 6–8 teachers, meet weekly to address student needs, guided by questions derived from PLC and RTI at Work. The schoolwide teams also meet weekly to support collaborative teacher teams and ensure that students requiring supplemental supports are progressing toward higher levels of learning.

The K–2 team uses curriculum-based measurements to benchmark and monitor early reading skills. An informal reading inventory is administered in grades 3–8 to benchmark and monitor reading accuracy, fluency, and comprehension. Computer-based assessments efficiently benchmark and monitor the current levels of performance of second through eighth graders in reading and mathematics.

Ninety percent of students at Robinson Elementary are eligible to receive free or reduced-price lunch, and 80 percent are designated as English learners. Across all grade levels, teachers spend at least ninety minutes on English language arts, seventy-five minutes on mathematics, and thirty minutes on English language development.

The K–2 collaborative teacher team and the schoolwide teams had concerns regarding Armando a year ago, when he was in kindergarten. These concerns centered on his immaturity and deficits in social skills. While curriculum-based measurements revealed initial difficulties in phonological awareness, specifically when asked to identify phonemes at the beginning of words, as well as when asked to segment and manipulate phonemes when prompted orally, Armando made steady progress when provided with differentiated Tier 1 instruction by his classroom teachers and with Tier 2 differentiated supports by the K–2 team. Targeted behavior supports allowed Armando to access instruction, although most of his supports were provided in small groups. Armando experienced limited success working with greater levels of independence. Armando had more reading success when presented with words on a page; his phonics skills, while initially below expected levels, progressed at a greater rate than his phonological skills. His comprehension abilities were adequate when provided with structured or oral supports. Inattentiveness seemed to compromise his skills at making meaning of text when reading independently or with oral supports. Armando's overall difficulties with fine motor skills inhibited his writing. Forming legible letters did not come easily, writing grip was a struggle, and he did not enjoy activities that involved, or necessitated, writing. The physical difficulties he experienced with writing, and the resulting dislike he developed of writing, led to Armando producing less writing, and his writing products lagged in quality behind those of his peers. While Armando eventually met counting and cardinality benchmarks, his difficulties applying early numeracy skills to more complex tasks depressed his mathematics achievement.

The increased cognitive and behavioral demands of first grade have made Armando's needs more pronounced. He continues to have difficulties with phonological awareness tasks, and his ability to process phonemes and other auditory inputs remains labored. These difficulties have extended to writing, where spelling words and other encoding skills are frustrating for Armando. Curriculum-based measurement scores that involve the identification, segmenting, and manipulation of phonemes remain well below expectations. His ability to decode pseudowords and actual words that include short vowels, long vowels, and consonant blends and digraphs is better than his phonological skills would predict. He can read preprimer texts that include visual supports with adequate levels of rate, accuracy, and prosody, although he still makes numerous errors when reading first-grade-level passages. His oral comprehension remains sound, but his continued difficulties reading text, and the fact that he reads fewer books than his peers, are beginning to impact his facility with employing comprehension techniques.

Armando does not like to write. Producing several sentences requires an extraordinary amount of time. The ideas and conventions, with the exception of spelling, within his writing reveal a promising ability to organize thoughts. Now that mathematics tasks require greater levels of reading and organization, Armando is falling behind his peers.

Armando is a young first grader, with an August birthday. Armando is the youngest child, and the next youngest is a seventh grader at Robinson Elementary. Armando's oldest brother and sister attend the district's high school. While Armando is energetic, he has not made close friends, and peers seem increasingly frustrated and confused by his difficulties in following rules, whether while playing or participating in classroom activities. The school has designed a system of supports to which Armando is adequately responding. He is making progress that is allowing him to access first-grade content. He is beginning to close the gap between his current levels of performance and the expected levels of first grade.

Katie and Wilson Elementary

Katie is a fourth-grade student at Wilson Elementary School, a large K–5 school of 756 students at the edge of a large city. Katie's teacher, Mr. Beyer, is one of five fourth-grade teachers at Wilson, and there are twenty-eight students in Katie's class. The members of Mr. Beyer's fourth-grade team collaborate weekly to cognitively plan instruction, design and select common assessments, analyze the efficacy of their instruction, and diagnose the needs of the fourth graders experiencing the most difficulty. They also design and deliver Tier 2 supports during a daily thirty-minute flex period, when the team is joined by one of the school's special education teachers.

There are thirty general education teachers at Wilson; they are joined by a reading specialist and two special education teachers, all three of whom meet with all students who are at risk, some with individualized education program (IEP) plans. The school has a principal and a dean who focus on students' social behaviors. With the school's social worker, the dean takes the lead on monitoring Tier 2 and 3 behavior supports. A psychologist, occupational therapist, speech and language pathologist, and registered nurse are on campus two days per week. Five paraprofessionals provide supplemental supports to all students who are at risk in small groups in all six grade levels, under the guidance of the reading specialist, frequently collaborating with collaborative teacher teams and the schoolwide leadership teams.

Over the past four years, staff have participated in high-quality professional development on PLCs, RTI, curriculum mapping, and building common assessments. Wilson is part of a 35,000-student school district and participates in districtwide PLC sessions four times a year.

Communication is a challenge in a school of 750 students and nearly 50 staff members, but Wilson leverages its staff in a collective effort to systematically meet student needs. Collaborative teacher teams at each grade level, with four or five teachers per team, meet at least once a week. Special education teachers work together as a collaborative teacher team, interacting, sharing, and communicating with grade-level teams at biweekly meetings held during common preps. Specials and elective teachers collaborate in person or virtually with content-alike teachers serving the district's other fifteen elementary schools. The schoolwide teams meet weekly to guide, lead, and sustain the PLC and RTI work. Intervention teams visit grade-level teams every three weeks for half an hour to problem solve (diagnose and prescribe) for students most at risk and those not yet responding to instruction and intervention. The intervention team meets with two grade-level teams per week.

Wilson staff administer curriculum-based measurements in reading to all students in grades K–5 three times a year. In addition, they use a computer-based adaptive test three times a year. The comprehensive, sixty-minute assessment tests students in reading and mathematics and allows for season-to-season comparisons due to its longitudinal scale. Teams have also selected, unpacked, and unwrapped essential standards, and have designed common assessments that are used to inform instruction.

Thirty percent of students at Wilson Elementary School qualify for free or reduced-price lunch and are categorized as socioeconomically disadvantaged. Twenty percent of students are designated as English learners. The school devotes 120 minutes per day to literacy and 90 minutes to mathematics.

Katie arrived at Wilson at the beginning of last school year, when she was starting third grade. Katie's father is a U.S. Marine, and he has been deployed overseas more than he has been at home over the past three years. Katie, her mom, and her little brother, a first-grade student at Wilson, move often. Katie is a sweet, very well-behaved child, compliant and shy. She has difficulty from time to time deeply comprehending texts she reads, either independently or with the rest of the class. Her fluency rate is low, but just within normal range. She makes fairly regular errors when she encounters multisyllabic words. While Katie's writing contains a few conventional errors, she writes and draws voluminously. Katie's sense of numbers and computational skills are solid. She occasionally needs a second explanation to master mathematics concepts. The larger areas of concern over the last year and a half are social-emotional in nature. Katie does not make friends easily. She is not organized, she neither self-regulates nor self-advocates, and she seems to lack motivation. The school's social worker began working with Katie and corresponding with Katie's mother at the end of her third-grade year.

Fourth grade has brought deterioration in Katie's social, emotional, and academic levels. While she remains a pleasant and cooperative girl, her grades are suffering, largely due to incomplete or missing assignments; her mastery of essential standards, predictably, is also showing an increasing number of gaps, although this does not seem to be due to significant academic skill deficits. She is reading less, which may be impacting her success at decoding more complex words and making meaning of more complex texts. She is writing as much as ever, and her mathematics performance is adequate, although she struggles when required to justify her answers through graphical or written explanations of her thinking and problem solving. Her social and emotional needs are most alarming, however.

Katie has withdrawn from the few friends she had started to make last year, although those friendships were not strong. She eats alone and walks aimlessly or sits and draws during recesses and breaks. Her teachers, the dean, the social worker, and the principal have all made it a priority to make positive contact with Katie every day but are discouraged that a breakthrough has not yet occurred; Katie has not opened up to any adult on campus. Katie's mom reports that her behavior is similar at home. She spends a lot of time alone and will lash out at her mother and brother seemingly without reason. And very recently, her teacher noticed small cuts on Katie's shins, just above her ankles. When asked about these cuts by her teacher, Katie withdrew and remained completely silent.

Holly and Roosevelt Elementary

Holly is a sixth-grade student in her last year at Roosevelt Elementary School. She has been receiving supports in the school district since she was three years of age. A normally sweet, compliant student, Holly spends most of her school day with Ms. Blackburn and a team of paraprofessionals. In fact, she has spent the last three years at Roosevelt with this team of educators. Holly was diagnosed with severe autism just before her third birthday. She is effectively mute. Ms. Blackburn and her team have helped Holly make great progress in academic and behavioral domains through intensive, targeted supports. They are currently planning for Holly's transition to junior high school.

Holly's mom and dad are divorced but are both regularly involved in Holly's school. They attend IEP meetings together, and Holly regularly spends time at her dad's house, although she lives with her mom, step-dad, and a younger step-brother and step-sister.

Roosevelt is a large, urban elementary school of 1,150 students. Three of the classes at Roosevelt serve students with severe and profound disabilities. Ms. Blackburn and her paraprofessional team meet frequently with the teams from the other two classes. They have designed a set of supports for students and their highly individualized literacy and numeracy needs. This special education team has participated in, and led, professional development for the entire staff in both programs and sets of strategies to ensure that students with significant deficits achieve at increasingly high levels. These professionals have also developed expertise in helping support students with severe behavioral challenges. Holly and her classmates experience behavioral challenges in the areas of socially appropriate actions, as well as in the visual-perceptual and sensory-processing domains. Significantly, Ms. Blackburn and other members of her collaborative teacher team have provided regular support and guidance to the rest of the Roosevelt staff; general education teachers also have students with these types of needs, albeit typically at a less intensive level. These collaborative efforts have strengthened staff practices for students with unique learning needs and have led to opportunities for inclusive practices.

Holly is mainstreamed into sixth-grade classes during electives, such as art and technology, and during physical education, and she partially participates in other core classes. A member of Ms. Blackburn's paraprofessional team joins Holly and her classmates during these opportunities. Holly also serves as a student office aide three days a week and works with a sixth-grade student buddy on an iPad 2 nearly every day of the week. Holly and her student buddy, Caroline, complete social-skills scenarios using a popular app.

Ms. Blackburn's team has assisted the Roosevelt staff in their understanding and application of RTI. As Ms. Blackburn explains, most everything that occurs in her classroom is designed to determine the extent to which students respond to various tasks. While this stimulus-response classroom design and the highly individualized nature of almost all instruction and assessment are not completely transferable to general education settings, general education and special education staff, led by Ms. Blackburn, have worked together to increasingly differentiate the time and support that different groups of students need. The general education staff recognize that they will never have the paraprofessional team that is required when working with students with severe and profound disabilities, but they are open to different ways of organizing the classroom and their instruction.

Forty percent of students at Roosevelt Elementary School are eligible for free or reduced-price lunch, and 25 percent are designated as English learners. In addition to the three classrooms for students with severe and profound disabilities, there are three special education teachers who serve students with mild and moderate disabilities. There are a total of forty general education teachers on campus, along with a principal, assistant principal, and guidance counselor.

Holly learned American Sign Language at an early age, and all teaching and learning with Holly occur through this medium. In preschool and early elementary school, Holly occasionally exhibited episodes of self-injurious and aggressive behaviors. While these types of difficulties have all but disappeared, changes of environment, such as the upcoming transition to the junior high, may result in a temporary reoccurrence.

Holly has displayed self-stemming behaviors since she was a toddler. These behaviors, which include hand flapping, spinning, and rocking, still occur, typically when Holly is presented with a new cognitive task or when she enters a new physical environment. She neither initiates interactions with others nor engages in play or dialogue when in a group. In mid-elementary school, she began to respond to stimuli both consistently and appropriately. She began to read preprimer texts in late elementary school, through instruction using a sight-word program called Edmark, and has continued to make steady progress in reading accuracy and rate with more complex texts. Her literal comprehension is average, but as of late elementary school, she has yet to demonstrate success in inferential comprehension.

While Holly's gross and fine motor skills have improved due to years of physical and occupational therapy, she continues to have difficulties with more complex physical tasks. Holly has had seizures in the past, although medical care has largely eliminated these epileptic-like occurrences.

Ms. Blackburn has been working on two interrelated goals this year: increasing Holly's literacy skills and her numeracy skills to complement her functional skills. In addition to receiving supports in reading more diverse and complex types of texts with greater comprehension and increasing her sense, and practical knowledge, of numbers, she participates in weekly, half-day field trips.

Holly has taken field trips to the junior high school she will attend and to various locales within the city. Holly makes these trips with a paraprofessional and other sixth-grade students from Roosevelt. The goal is a smooth transition into a productive, academically and functionally focused program at the junior high school next year.

Franklin and Middletown Middle School

Franklin is an academically gifted eighth-grade student, but he is often bored with school and rarely challenged by academic expectations. He is a popular student but does not enjoy working with others on group projects as he feels this will only lower the quality of his work. His popularity stems from his acting-out behavior in class that often results in him being asked to leave the room and report to the office. He is very much the class clown, and his biggest challenge is around organization as it relates to work completion. He is not prepared to "simply complete assignments" if they appear to be "busywork."

Middletown Middle School (MMS) is a grade 7–9 school serving approximately 750 students in a rural community. It's the only middle school in town, and the next closest middle school is two hours away in a neighboring school district. The school performs at an adequate level and has avoided external consequences. It's good enough to meet expectations but average enough to not exceed them. While Franklin knows he has the ability to excel in public school and beyond, he does not have plans to pursue a college degree and is not overly excited about attending high school. He feels that he learns more on his own than in the structured environment of school.

Many of the staff have been at MMS their entire careers and have seen a full range of students pass through the doors. They are confident about the programs they offer at school and support students outside of class time by sponsoring a variety of activities. Informally, a number of them provide additional academic supports to students, but neither systematically nor driven by common assessments. Franklin is not interested in attending tutorials, and staff members are not interested in his disruptive influence within them.

Students like Franklin appear to be increasing in number, and some staff members have asked for this to be a conversation topic at staff meetings, resulting in the establishment of smaller pods of students in all three grades. The pod model identifies students at each grade level who struggle academically or behaviorally and groups them together with positive role models and additional adult support. The school is large enough to have eight pods at each grade level; one pod at each grade has a maximum of eight students, all of whom have unique needs. The staff fully endorsed the model and were prepared to track data and use their collaboration time to further discuss the results and adjust planning as necessary.

The staff also agreed to implement a schoolwide system of universal screening assessments, common formative and summative assessments across the eight divisions in each grade, and behavioral progress-monitoring tools. Additionally, the staff have committed to learning more about functional behavioral assessments to get at the root cause of the noncompliant academic behaviors they are tracking.

Of the 750 students at MMS, 30 percent leave for the high school deficient in at least one core content area (English, mathematics, science, or social studies), and this has placed a burden on the resources at the high school. Students are often labeled "special education" or are placed on a waiting list for a formal evaluation. Some complete their three years at the high school without receiving any supplemental supports.

Franklin breezed through his elementary school and was considered a pleasant student with strong academic skills. The only concern noted was that he occasionally wandered mentally and did not always put his best effort into assignments. His elementary school was one of the smallest of the seven that funneled into MMS, and all his teachers and his small group of peers knew him; many had been together their entire elementary school careers.

When Franklin entered MMS, he met many new students and was assigned a different teacher for each subject. Moving from a small elementary school of one hundred students provided some challenges he had not experienced, while also providing a new audience. Early in grade 7, Franklin was sent out of class for questioning the validity of a teacher's response. Rather than being distraught, he enjoyed the experience that came with all eyes being on him and reveled in the laughter at his challenge of the teacher.

Anna and Heartland High School

Anna is an upbeat and outgoing tenth-grade student whose parents, due to military employment issues, have moved frequently, and as a result, Anna has attended five different schools growing up. Anna has multiple cognitive and physical disabilities that hamper her ability to access the typical school curriculum and has had trouble connecting with her grade-level peers in the past. Though Anna's cognitive functioning is low, she is aware of her inability to build close relationships with her peers, a dynamic magnified due to her transient upbringing and physical impairments.

Heartland High School (HHS) is a high-performing comprehensive high school serving approximately 750 students in a semirural Midwestern community. Consistency in schooling is a challenge for other students and families at HHS, as the school serves a local U.S. Air Force base in addition to its local population. Due to the transient nature of this segment of the school community, many times students arrive with gaps in their learning caused by frequent moves and attendance in a variety of school systems both in the United States and abroad.

After a number of initiatives (both state and district driven) had come and gone, it was decided that PLC with RTI was the best method to improve learning for all students at HHS, including Anna. As a result, a PLC structure was established three years ago to ensure a guaranteed and viable curriculum, quality assessment practices, and collective responsibility for maximizing high levels of learning for all students. HHS staff embraced the PLC model and adapted quickly to the use of data to drive decision making and timely student interventions. In unison with the implementation of the PLC model, the school implemented a robust professional development effort to ensure all faculty members would be well versed in research-based best practices in teaching and evidence-based decision making.

To further support both the whole-school PLC and course-alike teams and to help organize interventions, the schoolwide intervention team (SIT) supports each collaborative teacher team. The SIT members meet twice monthly to review progress and facilitate interventions for students who have been identified by universal screening measures or brought to their attention by collaborative teacher teams. The SIT helps to create, organize, and implement multitiered interventions for students based on their academic and behavioral progress in the classroom.

Both qualitative and quantitative data indicate that student learning has increased across all segments of the school population since the implementation of the PLC model and the use of RTI protocols. An extensive system of universal screening assessments, common formative and summative assessments, and progress-monitoring tools has been incorporated to provide timely feedback regarding student progress in learning. More individualized diagnostic testing is conducted for students on an as-needed basis.

Of the 750 students at HHS, 21 percent are receiving learning support services for functional learning deficiencies, physical disabilities, English learner status, or identified learning disabilities.

Anna is a student who presents significant physical, behavioral, and cognitive difficulties. Her physical handicaps were present at birth and consist of a palsied left side of her body. This lack of control causes drooping facial features, speech difficulties, belabored walking, and occasional incontinence that she now self-manages.

As a kindergarten student in the United States, Anna had been placed on an IEP. She responded well to initial intervention efforts, but due to her parents' jobs with the military, she moved overseas midway through her first-grade year. Though each school attempted to provide assistance to Anna, her disabilities, the inconsistency of intervention attempts, and varied school quality found her falling further and further behind her peers.

Due to Anna's challenging mental state, her parents decided to homeschool her during her ninth-grade year. This made connecting with peers even more difficult for Anna, causing her bouts of depression throughout her time away from school. Though Anna's parents attempted to connect her with activities outside of school and supported her through weekly counseling, Anna still struggled with isolation and disconnection from her peers.

Finally, before her tenth-grade school year, Anna's parents moved near HHS. By that time, Anna was in a state of despair. Her reading fluency and comprehension were very low, her math skills were at a third-grade level, and her physical handicaps made it increasingly difficult to connect with her peers, at times even resulting in her being bullied. Anna was tired of being the "kid who couldn't read," always being in the "special" classes, and being the last person to be chosen for activities, if she was chosen at all. By assessment standards, Anna was not the smartest student in the class, but she understood full well what it felt like to be the class outcast.

Upon entering HHS, Anna was given an adaptive computer-based assessment to provide a norm-referenced measure of her abilities. Anna scored below the tenth percentile in every academic category. As a result of her initial screening results, the HHS psychologist assessed Anna using precise diagnostic tests to more accurately define her reading deficits, math abilities, and general cognitive functioning. When Anna was given these long, nationally normed assessments, she was respectfully defiant and refused to give full effort on her assessments. Through years of testing, Anna had become "test shy." As a result, the school psychologist put in more time with Anna to build a solid relationship, using more personal assessment measures, such as the Qualitative Reading Inventory (QRI).

After significant staff-to-student relationship building, thoughtful testing procedures, and discussion among the HHS SIT, it was determined that Anna would require Tier 1, 2, and 3 supports. Anna's placement into a Tier 3 intervention meant that she would have immediate access to a case manager, a speech therapist, an occupational therapist, and small-group pullout instruction.

Throughout the rest of this book, we will return to our five students, describing how their schools embraced the four essential guiding principles of simplifying RTI to ensure high levels of learning.

Before returning to these students, however, we share a series of protocols and problem-solving tools that will help teams systematize supports on behalf of all students.

CHAPTER 3

Protocols and Problem Solving

The five students introduced in the previous chapter—Armando, Katie, Holly, Franklin, and Anna—are not atypical. Virtually every school has students with similar needs. Yet, like a fingerprint, each of these students is distinctly unique—a singular combination of academic skills and behaviors, shaped by his or her individual aptitudes and previous experiences, and motivated by his or her own needs, wants, and dreams. Likewise, the school that each student attends is similar to thousands of schools across the nation, yet unique in the combination of skills and expertise of the collective school staff and the specific resources available to support student learning. Because no two students or schools are exactly alike, it would be naïve to expect broad federal guidelines, universal state regulations, predetermined district protocols, or commercially produced intervention programs alone to successfully determine and monitor interventions that must be tailored to the individual academic and behavioral needs of each student.

Unfortunately, we see many schools and districts approach interventions with either an exclusively protocol-driven process that fails to consider the unique combination of symptoms and causes demonstrated by each student, or a problem-solving model that lacks the systematic safeguards necessary to ensure that every student who needs additional help gets it. Like the chicken-or-egg dilemma, successfully responding when students need additional support does not require either schoolwide protocols designed to classify student needs into predetermined interventions *or* a problem-solving process designed to dig deeply into the individual needs of each student needing extra help. It takes protocols *and* problem-solving processes—a "pro-solve" process—as protocols create an effective, systematic process to ensure that students' access to schoolwide interventions is not dependent on the teacher(s) to which they are assigned, and problem-solving enables a school to tailor its collective efforts to the unique needs of each student. In this chapter, we will describe an integrated pro-solve process to identify a student's academic and behavioral needs, determine interventions, and establish specific staff responsibilities to successfully implement and monitor the plan.

The Pro-Solve Intervention Targeting Process

Determining the appropriate academic and behavior interventions for an individual student requires a highly effective problem-solving process. This process must identify not only the obstacles that are hindering a student's success, but also the causes of these hurdles, the best interventions to address these needs, the desired outcomes, and who will be the lead person or team responsible for carrying out each intervention. These goals are captured in the RTI at Work Pro-Solve Intervention Targeting Process outlined in figure 3.1.

At the heart of the protocol is a sequence of five critical questions that helps determine the causes and potential solutions for a student in need of academic and behavior interventions. These powerful questions include:

1. **What is/are the concern(s)?:** Obviously, it is unlikely a student would be referred for interventions unless there is at least one concern regarding the student's current level of achievement. Because students struggle because of both academic and behavioral needs, consider both skill and will concerns.

2. **What is/are the cause(s) of the concern(s)?:** Many struggling students demonstrate the same academic and behavioral concerns, such as low test scores, poor grades, inconsistent attendance, missing assignments, and disruptive behavior. It is critical to remember that these concerns represent similar symptoms, but the underlying causes can vary from student to student. For example, poor attendance can be a concern numerous students in need of interventions demonstrate, but this does not mean the cause of each student's absences is the same. The key is to determine why each student is missing school. Eliminate the cause, and solve the problem.

3. **What is/are the desired outcome(s)?:** Many schools fall into the trap of focusing on eliminating the negative concern, instead of targeting the desired positive outcomes. For example, the concern might be that a student demonstrates disruptive behavior by inappropriately blurting out answers

Student: _____ **Meeting Date:** _____

Participants: _____

	1. Concern	2. Cause	3. Desired Outcomes	4. Intervention Steps	5. Who Takes Responsibility
Led by Teacher Teams					
Led by Schoolwide Teams					

Next Meeting Date: _____

Figure 3.1: RTI at Work pro-solve intervention targeting process.

*Visit **go.solution-tree.com/rtiatwork** for a reproducible version of this figure.*

during whole-group instruction. Instead of discussing what steps the school staff can take to stop the disruptive behavior, a better discussion would be to determine the appropriate academic behaviors that the student must learn to successfully participate in whole-group learning opportunities.

4. **What steps should be taken to best achieve the desired outcome(s)?:** By moving beyond assigning students to interventions based on common symptoms and instead diagnosing the cause of each student's struggles and then determining the desired positive outcomes, the school is now ready to identify the interventions and action steps necessary to meet a specific student's needs.

5. **Who is going to take lead responsibility to ensure that each intervention is implemented?:** The best-made plans are useless if they are not effectively implemented. Yet, when everyone is responsible for an intervention, no one is responsible. At some point, the buck must stop with someone to ensure an intervention moves from a plan to action.

This five-step pro-solve targeting process is the same for both supplemental and intensive interventions, but the curricular outcomes and problem-solving teams are different between Tier 2 and Tier 3. The need for these differences is captured in the RTI at Work pyramid.

Examining the RTI at Work Pyramid

As we explained in the introduction, RTI and PBIS researchers have used the shape of a pyramid to visually capture a system of tiered interventions. When used properly, this graphic is a useful approach to assist in organizing a school's core instruction and support resources. Unfortunately, we frequently see three dangerous misinterpretations of this graphic. The first is when schools view the pyramid as primarily a new way to qualify students for special education, making the tiers merely new hoops that a school must jump through prior to placing students into traditional special education services. This incorrect application is understandable, as the traditional pyramid seems to focus a school's intervention system toward one point: special education. In the end, this approach tends to become a self-fulfilling prophecy because the organization started interventions with protocols designed to screen and document students for this potential outcome.

To address this detrimental view of the traditional pyramid, we intentionally inverted the RTI at Work pyramid, visually focusing a school's interventions on a single point: the individual child (figure 3.2).

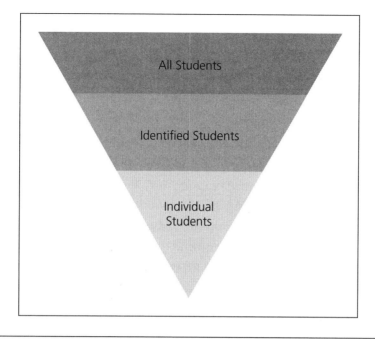

All Students

Identified Students

Individual
Students

Figure 3.2: RTI inverted pyramid.

With this approach, the school begins the intervention process assuming that every
student is capable of learning at high levels. Because not every student learns the
same way, learns at the same speed, or enters school with the same prior access to
learning, core instruction alone will not be sufficient to meet the learning needs of
every child. If the school can provide targeted instruction and additional time to
learn, every child can succeed.

The second misinterpretation is when schools view Tier 1 as the responsibility of
classroom teachers, and supplemental and intensive intervention as the responsibility
of interventionist staff, such as instructional aides, categorical-funded teachers, and
special education staff. This approach reinforces a belief in general education teachers
that they are responsible only for initial teaching. If students require help after initial
teaching, the classroom teacher's response is, Who do I send them to? Especially at
schools with a large number of at-risk students, this practice overwhelms the intervention team, site intervention resources, and the RTI process.

In response to this problem, many districts dictate that classroom teachers cannot
refer a student for schoolwide interventions until they can document a set of predetermined interventions that must first be tried in the classroom. This mandate places
the initial response of Tier 2 interventions with classroom teachers. The problem
with this approach is that every student does not struggle for the same reason. As
we have discussed in the previous chapters, the reasons can vary from just needing

a little extra practice on a new concept, to lacking necessary prerequisite skills, to requiring assistance with English language, to attendance and behavioral issues. It is unlikely that each teacher has all the skills and time needed to effectively meet every need, making some initial Tier 2 responses an impossible responsibility for classroom teachers. This approach fails students *and* educators.

The answer lies not in determining who is responsible for intervening when students don't learn after core instruction—classroom teachers *or* the school's intervention resources—but in determining the responsibilities of these specific groups to ensure that *all* students succeed. To visually capture this thinking, we have divided the RTI at Work pyramid into two distinct areas of responsibility: interventions led by collaborative teacher teams and interventions led by the school leadership and intervention teams (figure 3.3). At Tier 2, we recommend that teacher teams take the lead in skill interventions, while schoolwide resources take the lead in will interventions.

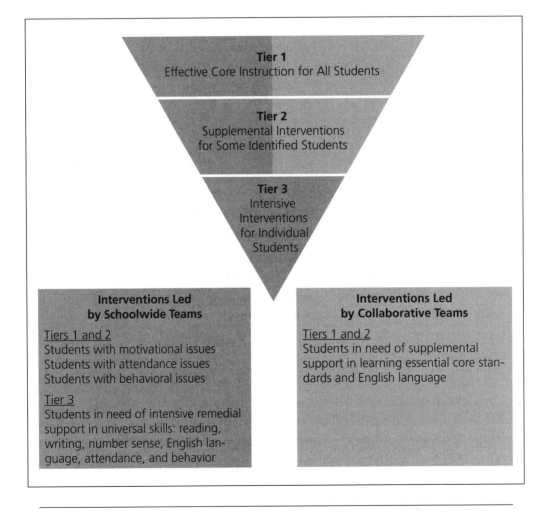

Figure 3.3: The RTI at Work pyramid.

The final misapplication of the traditional pyramid is when schools interpret the difference between the tiers exclusively as an increase in instructional intensity. This approach generally focuses on providing tiered interventions that increase in the duration and frequency of instruction, while lowering the teacher-to-student ratio as a student moves "up" the pyramid. Regrettably, to achieve this goal at Tier 3, students are often removed from essential grade-level curriculum and placed in remedial coursework, virtually ensuring that these students will continue to achieve below grade level.

While we certainly agree that interventions should become more targeted and intensive as students demonstrate the need, the ultimate goal of any intervention is to close achievement gaps to ensure that all students learn at grade level or higher. To achieve this outcome, the tiers represent not only an increase in instructional intensity, but also a distinct difference in the desired learning outcomes, as shown in figure 3.4 (page 50).

In the RTI at Work pyramid, Tier 1 represents more than effective initial instruction; it also represents the curricular goal of providing all students access to the absolutely essential grade-level academic and behavioral expectations that must be mastered to properly prepare students for the next grade level and beyond.

Because we know not every student will have learned these essential academic and behavioral learning outcomes after initial instruction, the school must provide more targeted supplemental instruction at Tier 2 to ensure all students gain these essential Tier 1 learning outcomes. It is also highly likely that not every student will enter each school year having fully mastered all the immediate prerequisite academic and behavioral skills necessary to succeed in new grade-level expectations. Subsequently, a school will use supplemental intervention time to fill these specific learning gaps. Most importantly, students in need of Tier 2 interventions must not miss Tier 1 instruction of new essential standards. Instead, this supplemental support will be provided in addition to the Tier 1 core—"the core *and* more."

Applying the Pro-Solve Process to Tier 1 and Tier 2

Because the curricular goals at Tier 1 and Tier 2 focus on essential grade-level academic and behavioral standards and the immediate prerequisite skills that the grade-level standards are built on, interventions for these tiers should provide students additional time and support to master these outcomes. And since every student in need of extra help will not struggle for the same reason, the pro-solve process can be used to target each student's particular needs for both skill and will. These curricular outcomes and the pro-solve process have been combined to create the Tier 1/Tier 2

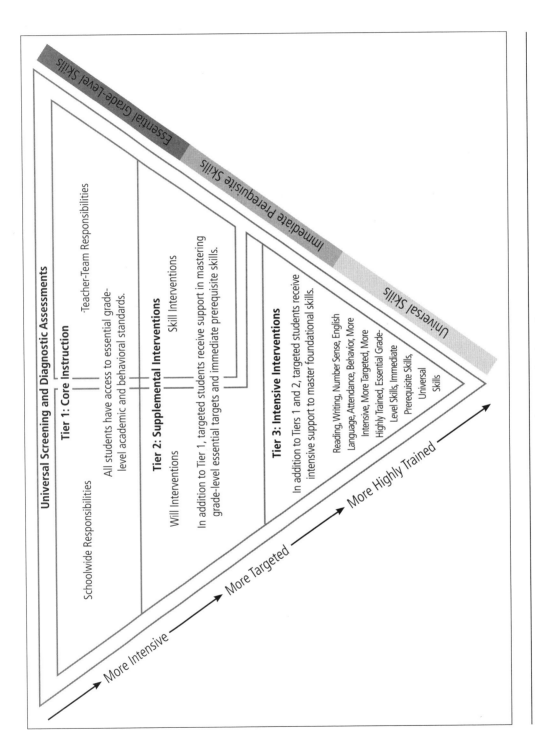

Figure 3.4: The RTI at Work pyramid with learning outcomes and intervention intensity.

*Visit **go.solution-tree.com/rtiatwork** for a reproducible version of this figure.*

Intervention Targeting and Monitoring Process, as shown in figure 3.5 (page 51) and 3.6 (page 53). These tools are designed to provide clarity about which team should take primary responsibility for leading specific types of skill and will interventions.

Because this targeting process combines skill and will interventions, participation in completing the process and implementing the recommendations must include the individuals most responsible for meeting the academic needs of the targeted student at Tier 1 and the individuals who lead the schoolwide behavior supports. Specifically, we recommend that the following teams participate and take lead responsibility in the following areas of need.

Collaborative Teacher Team Responsibilities

Collaborative teacher teams take lead responsibility in determining essential academic standards, providing initial instruction, and assessing student progress toward meeting these critical learning outcomes. For this reason, they are the professionals best positioned to take lead responsibility for the following Tier 2 academic interventions.

- **Grade-level essential standards**: These are the academic skills and knowledge that the teacher team has identified as absolutely essential for every student to master to be adequately prepared for success in the next course or grade level.

- **Immediate prerequisite skills**: These are the specific academic skills and knowledge that represent the immediate building blocks to grade-level essential standards. They were most likely taught either in a previous unit, in a previous school year, or in the previous course within a subject-based sequence of coursework.

- **English language**: At Tier 2, students who need support in English language have already learned basic conversational English but might still need assistance with subject-specific academic vocabulary and the written structures of English.

Schoolwide Team Responsibilities

While teacher teams lead on the preceding skill interventions, the leadership team will coordinate the school's support resources to take the lead in the following supplemental behavior interventions.

- **Academic behaviors**: School support staff can help students who need assistance in academic behaviors, such as completion of assignments, study skills and organization, staying focused and on task, and appropriate classroom participation.

- **Social behaviors**: Interventions in social behaviors can include assistance with school attendance, positive peer relationships,

Student: _____   **Meeting Date:** _____

Participants: _____

Targeted Outcomes		1. Concern	2. Cause	3. Desired Outcomes	4. Intervention Steps	5. Who Takes Responsibility
Led by Teacher Teams	Grade-level essential standards					
	Immediate prerequisite skills					
	English language					
Led by Schoolwide Teams	Academic behaviors					
	Social behaviors					
	Health and home					

Next Meeting Date: _____

Figure 3.5: RTI at Work pro-solve intervention targeting process—Tier 1 and Tier 2.

*Visit **go.solution-tree.com/rtiatwork** for a reproducible version of this figure.*

Student: _____   **Meeting Date:** _____

Participants: _____

	Targeted Outcomes	Desired Outcomes	Intervention and Action Steps	Who	Data Point 1	Data Point 2	Data Point 3	Data Point 4	Data Point 5
Led by Teacher Teams	Essential standards								
	Immediate prerequisite skills								
	English language								
Led by Schoolwide Teams	Academic behaviors								
	Social behaviors								
	Health and home								

Next Meeting Date: _____

Figure 3.6: RTI at Work pro-solve intervention monitoring plan—Tier 1 and Tier 2.

*Visit **go.solution-tree.com/rtiatwork** for a reproducible version of this figure.*

sportsmanship in competitive activities, and appropriate school language.

- **Health and home:** Sometimes specific health concerns and home factors can negatively affect student achievement in school, such as a student who might miss class time due to a mild bout of asthma caused by a windy day, or a child upset at school because his or her parent is soon to be deployed for military duty. The school's health and counseling staff could provide supplemental support, thus helping the student attend and stay focused in class.

We recommend that a school has a systematic process, approximately every three weeks, in which students are identified who might need Tier 2 supports in these academic and behavioral areas. By *systematic*, we mean that it should not matter which teacher a student is assigned to for core instruction—if the student would benefit from supplemental help, the school can guarantee that the student will be identified for this pro-solve process.

While the pro-solve targeting process is designed to effectively determine a student's needs, identify effective interventions, and assign responsibilities for carrying out the intervention plan, it is unlikely that initial results will create a perfect intervention plan. Once an intervention plan is developed, team members must monitor student progress to determine if the desired outcomes are being achieved. If the student is responding and the interventions are working, then share high fives; if the student is not responding, the intervention team must revise the plan based on the updated information gathered through the monitoring process. Either way, monitoring a student's response to the additional support is required.

Putting the *R* in RTI

Progress-monitoring is a critical component of simplifying RTI. Simply stated, there is no RTI unless we know the extent to which students are responding. The process of monitoring a student's response to instruction and intervention and the evidence that is produced and collaboratively analyzed represent a significant juncture in a team's problem-solving process regarding a student.

- Is the student responding adequately to supports?
- Does the student's progress mean that supports can be reduced or discontinued?
- What does the student's lack of progress reveal about the student's needs, and how can interventions be more targeted and successful?

Progress-monitoring can be most simply explained and efficiently conducted by describing how we uniquely monitor a student's response to Tier 2, Tier 3, and behavior interventions. Progress-monitoring has seemed to stump many schools; teams can't seem to find the right monitoring tool, progress-monitoring is confusing, or monitoring does not produce useful results. We feel, however, that the problem lies not with the progress-monitoring tool but with the "targetedness" of the intervention. The more targeted the intervention, the more successful the intervention. Moreover, when we are as clear as possible about the specific areas of student need—about the specific focus of intervention—the type of monitoring tool we use will logically emerge.

Tier 2 Progress-monitoring

Teams identify students who have not yet mastered essential standards through their collaborative administration and analysis of common assessments. These collaborative analyses reveal more than which students require additional time and alternative strategies to learn at high levels; they also provide evidence regarding the specific learning targets with which students require this supplemental support. In planning for their collective response, teams also collaboratively examine which team member has had the greatest levels of relative success in helping students master the grade-level or course essentials. A sample Tier 2 progress-monitoring form for grade 8 ELA is shown in figure 3.7 (page 56).

Given the process that teams use to prepare, plan, and provide Tier 2 interventions, the assessment that teams should use to monitor student progress—to assess students' response to intervention—is logical. Teams should use alternate items from the very same common assessments that revealed specific student needs in the first place. We need not readminister an entire alternate version of the common assessment— just those items for which the student did not demonstrate mastery and for which he or she received Tier 2 support. Let's not overcomplicate RTI. We use common assessments to measure student learning of essentials after Tier 1 instruction. Tier 2 supports are designed to provide students who are in need with more time and alternative strategies to master Tier 1 essentials; we should use alternate items from common assessments to monitor progress of these supports.

Behavior and Attendance Progress-monitoring

When a student's behavior is impacting academic and school success, teams must first determine the causes of student misbehavior using a tool such as a simplified functional behavioral analysis (FBA). A collaborative examination of the antecedents or causes of misbehavior will allow teams to help students improve specific behavioral skills with specific behavioral strategies. We measure a student's response to these interventions—monitoring student progress in the areas of behavior and attendance—using a research-based process known as check-in/check-out (CI/CO) and the tool in figure 3.8 (pages 57–58).

CCSS	Description	Mastery
Literature		
RL.8.1	Cite the textual evidence that most strongly supports an analysis of what the text says explicitly, as well as inferences drawn from the text.	
RL.8.2	Determine a theme or central idea of a text and analyze its development over the course of the text, including its relationship to the characters, setting, and plot; provide an objective summary of the text.	
RL.8.3	Analyze how particular lines of dialogue or incidents in a story or drama propel the action, reveal aspects of a character, or provoke a decision.	
RL.8.4	Determine the meaning of words and phrases as they are used in a text, including figurative and connotative meanings; analyze the impact of specific word choices on meaning and tone, including analogies or allusions to other texts.	
RL.8.5	Compare and contrast the structure of two or more texts, and analyze how the differing structure of each text contributes to its meaning and style.	
RL.8.6	Analyze how differences in the points of view of the characters and the audience or reader (e.g., created through the use of dramatic irony) create such effects as suspense or humor.	
RL.8.7	Analyze the extent to which a filmed or live production of a story or drama stays faithful to or departs from the text or script, evaluating the choices made by the director or actors.	
RL.8.9	Analyze how a modern work of fiction draws on themes, patterns of events, or character types from myths, traditional stories, or religious works such as the Bible, including describing how the material is rendered new.	
RL.8.10	By the end of the year, read and comprehend literature, including stories, dramas, and poems, at the high end of the grades 6–8 text complexity band independently and proficiently.	
Informational Text		
RI.8.1	Cite the textual evidence that most strongly supports an analysis of what the text says explicitly, as well as inferences drawn from the text.	
RI.8.2	Determine a central idea of a text and analyze its development over the course of the text, including its relationship to supporting ideas; provide an objective summary of the text.	
RI.8.3	Analyze how a text makes connections among and distinctions between individuals, ideas, or events (e.g., through comparisons, analogies, or categories).	

Figure 3.7: Tier 2 progress-monitoring form for grade 8 ELA.

CI/CO is both a monitoring and a mentoring tool. First, though, we must ensure that the target behavior has been determined, that a strategy to improve the target behavior has been identified, and that the student and all staff who work with the student understand the target behavior and strategy. Under these conditions, CI/CO is a simple, powerful monitoring tool.

CI/CO produces timely data that can be used to measure the effectiveness of the strategy and student progress. Students are intentionally involved in monitoring their behavior, and mentoring builds the relationships and provides the guidance and feedback that will contribute to improved habits and behaviors. This same CI/CO monitoring procedure can be used to monitor and mentor student progress with attendance.

The type of progress-monitoring tool should relate to the type of interventions that we are providing and the types of skills we are addressing. Table 3.1 (page 59) shows the type of progress being monitored along with the type of tool.

Monitoring Through CI/CO

Check-in: "How was your afternoon? How many points did you earn yesterday? What was one thing that went well yesterday? What was one thing that could have gone better? What is your goal for today? Have a great day, and good luck on your math test. See you after school."

Check-in/check-out for: _____

Check-in/check-out with: _____

Date: _____

Today, I am working on: _____

This is how I did today:
3 = Great!   (I was reminded to be on task 1 or 0 times.)
2 = Pretty good   (I was reminded to be on task 3 or 2 times.)
1 = So-so   (I was reminded to be on task more than 3 times.)

Specific and measurable goal: _____

Students monitor, evaluate, and score their behavior first.

Continued →

Figure 3.8: Monitoring through CI/CO.

Times of the Day	Staying on Task	
	Student	Staff

Today I earned _____ points.

Students are working toward a positive reinforcer. The goal should increase with greater levels of success before ultimately removing the positive reinforcer. Student and staff scores and progress toward the goal are reviewed at check-out.

_____ points or more = _____

*Visit **go.solution-tree.com/rtiatwork** for a reproducible version of this figure.*

Table 3.1: Types of Progress-monitoring and Tools

Type of Progress Being Monitored	Type of Progress-Monitoring Tool
Progress in response to Tier 2 interventions	Alternate versions of common assessments
Progress in response to Tier 3 interventions	Curriculum-based measurements
Progress in response to behavior interventions	Check-in/check-out procedures

The success of progress-monitoring is dependent on the targetedness of the monitoring, which in turn is dependent on the targetedness of the interventions themselves. When students are involved in the monitoring and goal-setting processes, progress-monitoring can shift from being a burden to being a powerful component of RTI at Work.

Using the supplemental pro-solve and progress-monitoring tools, let's apply these processes to each of our students—Armando, Katie, Holly, Franklin, and Anna—to provide a very detailed picture of how a school can address each of these students' skill and will needs.

CHAPTER 4

Uniting Core Instruction and Interventions

N ow that we have a common understanding of the essential guiding principles, visual framework, and targeting processes needed to create an effective systematic intervention process that addresses the needs of both skill and will, we can consider how these processes and tools can be applied to meet the unique needs of Armando, Katie, Holly, Franklin, and Anna.

Adopting Fundamental Assumptions

Prior to providing systematic interventions, each school needs to create the learning-focused culture, collaborative structures, instructional focus, and ongoing assessment processes required to successfully respond when students need additional time and support. By culture, we are referring to the norms, values, assumptions, and collective beliefs of each school. Successful interventions require each school to commit to two fundamental assumptions about Armando, Katie, Holly, Franklin, and Anna.

First, all school staff must assume that all students are capable of learning at high levels. There cannot be a sliding scale of student expectations that assumes students who come from parents who are economically stable, English speaking, actively involved, and highly educated are more capable of learning at high levels, while children who come from families that are economically disadvantaged, non–English speaking, uninvolved, and uneducated are less capable of meeting rigorous learning expectations. Across North America, minority students, English learners, and economically disadvantaged students are disproportionately represented in special education (Brantlinger, 2006; Ferri & Connor, 2006; Skiba et al., 2008, Skiba, Poloni-Staudinger, Gallini,

Simmons, & Feggins-Azziz, 2006) and underrepresented in gifted and honors programs (Donovan & Cross, 2002). Students perceived as being capable of learning at high levels are placed in more rigorous courses taught at advanced levels, are expected to achieve, and thus are much more likely to learn at this level. Conversely, students perceived as being incapable of learning at high levels are placed in below-grade-level curriculum, are taught at remedial levels, and are expected to achieve at lower levels, and to no one's surprise, they will most likely learn at low levels. These outcomes falsely confirm the school's initial assumptions and reinforce its misguided practices.

The second fundamental assumption of a school committed to a culture of collective responsibility is that the school staff accept responsibility for ensuring the high levels of learning for these students. While parental, societal, and economic forces impact student learning, the actions of educators will ultimately determine each child's success in school. There is no question that factors outside a school's control impact student learning, and it is understandable why educators can feel like victims of these factors. In his seminal work *Visible Learning*, John Hattie (2009) completed a meta-analysis of the factors that have the greatest impact on student learning, including both school and environmental factors. Of these factors, the first thirty most powerful influences are provided at school, while the highest home/environmental factor is number thirty-one (Hattie, 2009).

Fulfilling the obligations of collective responsibility requires more than the belief that all students can learn at high levels—it also requires the staff to work collaboratively to achieve this goal. To this end, teachers who share essential learning outcomes work in collaborative teams to ensure that their collective students master these standards. Working collaboratively is not only a desired outcome at each school, it is an expectation of every staff member. If the purpose of collective responsibility is to ensure that all students learn at high levels, then allowing any teacher to work in isolation would be unacceptable. (To dig deeper into collaborative practices and structures, we highly recommend the book *Learning by Doing* [DuFour et al., 2010].)

Concentrating Instruction

There is, perhaps, no greater obstacle to all students learning at the levels of depth and complexity necessary to graduate from high school ready for college or a skilled career than the overwhelmingly and inappropriately large number of standards that students are expected to master. They are so numerous, in fact, that teachers cannot even adequately *cover* them, let alone effectively teach them. Moreover, students are far too often diagnosed with a learning disability because we have proceeded through the curriculum (or pacing guide or textbook) too quickly. We do not build in time for the remediation and reteaching that we know some students will require; we do not focus our efforts on the most highly prioritized standards and ensure that students learn deeply, enduringly, and meaningfully.

Concentrating instruction signifies that we will collaborate and determine which standards are "must knows" and which standards are "nice to knows." This does not suggest that we will not teach all standards; rather, it guarantees that all students will learn the must-know standards because we will have developed a viable plan. To those who would suggest that all standards are important or that nonteachers can and should prioritize standards, we respectfully ask, "Will teachers feel a sense of ownership if they do not participate in this process? Will teachers understand why standards were prioritized? Will they stay faithful to first ensuring that all students master the must knows, or will teachers continue to determine their own priorities and preferences regarding what is taught in the privacy of their classroom, as they have for decades?"

Concentrating instruction also signifies that all teachers have the same interpretation of the meaning of standards. Collaborative teacher teams must interpret the "educationese" in which standards are written to provide the instruction that ensures students master the standards. The Essential Standards Chart in figure 4.1 (page 64) can guide teams in this process—a process that will guide instruction and instructional decisions while also informing the selection of common formative assessment items.

We draw upon the work of Reeves (2002) in prioritizing standards.

- Readiness: A standard is a clear prerequisite for the next grade level or course of study.

- Leverage: A standard represents thinking required in multiple grade levels.

- Endurance: A standard represents a 21st century and college or career readiness skill.

Once prioritized, collaborative teacher teams will determine the number of must-know standards that can be viably taught so that all students can deeply master them. This step often flexibly involves teams as teams place standards within maps or calendars that ultimately define units of study. Optimally, the concentrated instruction process for academic content is articulated vertically, from grade to grade or course to course.

The word *fidelity* continues to challenge our decisions when concentrating instruction. While we recognize the benefits of, and necessity for, curricular materials, we believe that fidelity to standards and student needs is the very best way of ensuring a guaranteed, viable curriculum.

			What Is It We Expect Students to Learn?			
Grade:		Subject:		Semester:	Team Members:	
Description of Standard	Example of Rigor	Prerequisite Skills	When Taught?	Common Summative Assessment	Extension Standards
What is the essential standard to be learned? Describe in student-friendly vocabulary.	What does proficient student work look like? Provide an example and/or description.	What prior knowledge, skills, and/or vocabulary are needed for a student to master this standard?	When will this standard be taught?	What assessment(s) will be used to measure student mastery?	What will we do when students have already learned this standard?

Source: Buffum et al., 2012, p. 72–73.

Figure 4.1: Essential standards chart.

*Visit **go.solution-tree.com/rtiatwork** for a reproducible of this figure.*

The process of prioritizing standards and concentrating instruction also applies to social and academic behaviors. In *Pyramid of Behavior Interventions: Seven Keys to a Positive Learning Environment* (Hierck et al., 2011), we describe these steps as:

1. Common expectations

    *   School rules, codes of conduct, and mission statements have been condensed into a few easy-to-remember, positively phrased common words or phrases.

    *   Behavioral expectations are linked to academic expectations.

    *   Students, staff, and parents know the expectations.

    *   Everyone in the school uses this common language.

    *   Kids know the expectations.

    *   Adults model the expectations.

2. Targeted instruction

    *   Schoolwide expectations are taught directly by all staff to all students, and in context (for example, appropriate lunchroom behavior is taught in the lunchroom).

    *   Students are given opportunities to develop, practice, and demonstrate appropriate social skills.

    *   Common expectations are reviewed regularly, practiced often, and recognized and rewarded when displayed correctly.

    *   Social skills are taught the same as academic skills: demonstrate, practice, review, and celebrate.

3. Positive reinforcement

    *   Catch kids being good. (Don't bribe.) Acknowledge them.

    *   Timely and specific feedback is critical to improved learning.

    *   The words we use can be as powerful as, or more powerful than, any tangible reinforcer. Words should promote a growth mindset and positivity.

    *   Reward the behavior, not the student.

- School staff members who are uncomfortable with tokens and rewards concentrate on recognizing students for displaying positive social and academic skills.

- Behaviors that we wish to see more commonly displayed are intentionally and systematically (in the same manner, at the same frequency, and for the same reasons) reinforced.

The Essential Standards Chart (figure 4.1, page 64) can guide the work of teams in academics, as well as social and academic behaviors.

Using Data

Common formative assessments (CFAs) are the tests that collaborative teacher teams use to ensure that students are mastering essential standards. When collaborative teacher teams analyze results on a by-the-student, by-the-standard, by-the-skill basis, they can determine who needs additional supports and the skills with which students most need that additional support. The more well designed the CFA, the more accurate the assessment; the more accurate the assessment, the more targeted the Tier 2 interventions will be.

While our accurate use of evidence to drive academic decisions can improve, a near-complete absence of evidence compromises our efforts in the area of behavior. The decisions that we make to establish and revise our behavior supports often lack the rationale that evidence can provide. We simply do not gather enough behavioral data. Through a simple process of recording, preserving, organizing, and analyzing data on major and minor incidents, schools can utilize the power of evidence and data-informed decision making in behavior, just as they effectively do in academics. The behavior documentation form in figure 4.2, when combined with a simple, inexpensive online data-warehousing system such as SWIS (School-Wide Information System), can provide schools with the tools that they require to converge assessments and information in the area of behavior.

To ensure that every student has access to the time and support he or she needs to learn at high levels, we recommend that school teams follow a systematic process: identify, determine, monitor, and revise/extend. When applied to Tier 1 supports, *identify* involves invoking the useful cliché, *If it's predictable, it's preventable.* We will discuss universal screening in later chapters as well; in Tier 1, universal screening information can reveal students who lack the foundational skills needed to access Tier 1 instruction in the absence of early, frequent, and intentional scaffolds and other differentiation strategies. When students cannot read at grade level,

Student name: _____   **Staff:** _____   **Date:** _____   **Time:** _____

Location: _____ classroom _____ walkway _____ library _____ restroom _____ playground _____ lunch area

Major:
_____ abusive/inappropriate language
_____ fighting/physical aggression
_____ defiance/disrespect/noncompliance
_____ lying/cheating
_____ harassment/bullying

_____ disruption
_____ truancy
_____ property damage
_____ forgery/theft
_____ use/possession of controlled substance/weapon

Minor:
_____ inappropriate language
_____ physical contact
_____ defiance/disrespect/noncompliance
_____ disruption

Follow-up action(s):
_____ no recess (_____ recess/days)
_____ conference with student
_____ parent contact
_____ privilege loss (_____)
_____ time in office
_____ in-house suspension (_____ days)
_____ out-of-school suspension (_____ days)
_____ other:

Return to classroom teacher.
Parent signature: _____

Comments:

Others involved:
_____ none
_____ staff
_____ teacher
_____ unknown
_____ peers (_____)

Motivation:
_____ obtain peer attention
_____ avoid task/activity
_____ don't know
_____ avoid peer
_____ obtain adult attention
_____ avoid adult
_____ obtain item/activity

Source: Buffum et al., 2012.

Figure 4.2: Sample school behavior documentation form.

*Visit **go.solution-tree.com/rtiatwork** for a reproducible version of this figure.*

their ability to practice comprehension during reading instruction is going to be impacted; they will require access to text at their instructional level to practice these skills. This same scenario will be repeated in other content areas. When students cannot effectively communicate their understanding in writing, they will not be able to demonstrate mastery in traditional ways; they will require alternative opportunities, such as oral, graphical, or technology-assisted ways of assessing their learning. When students' behaviors inhibit their ability to learn, engaging pedagogies can make a difference; strategies and supports that help students improve their behaviors will need to be consistently employed so that students are attentive and engaged in their learning.

Certain access in the area of Tier 1 behavior demands greater attention from most schools with which, and in which, we work. The keys to a positive learning environment identified earlier in this chapter—common expectations, targeted instruction, and positive reinforcement—must be consistently, systematically, and thoroughly present in every classroom, hallway, and common-use space in the school and must be modeled and supported and emphasized by every adult at all times. We will never evolve beyond complaining about student misbehavior unless we commit to ensuring that all students have access to core behavior supports, a goal that will only be realized by the enthusiastic participation of all staff.

We have questions and concerns about the practice of supplanting core, Tier 1 instruction. Do we demonstrate a belief in all students learning at high levels when we replace core instruction with intensive interventions? To state it simply: we believe in AND, not OR (Collins, 2005). Schools with which we work are increasingly providing students who are at risk with core instruction *and* intensive academic interventions. We recognize and accept that providing students instruction at their levels is an important element of the suite of supports required to improve student learning with a sense of urgency; we also understand the logistical difficulties associated with AND. However, there are simply too many costs, in our experiences, associated with supplanting core instruction with a replacement curriculum. Among these costs are (1) students who participate in a replacement program get the message that they are separate from their classmates, and (2) even when students make the dramatic gains that we hope for and expect when they receive these intensive supports, their transitions back into the core instructional environments are too infrequently smooth and successful.

We have similar concerns about schools' use of ability grouping (see Hattie [2009] for a review of ability grouping's research base). Again, do we demonstrate a belief in all students learning at high levels when we separate them based on ability levels? We believe in the power of heterogeneous student interactions and in differentiated instructional practices. An analogous and equally unfortunate practice is when schools provide support to special education students, as defined by IEP documents, when their general education classmates are receiving core instruction. These practices must be examined, and in our opinion changed, so that schools operationalize the beliefs articulated in their mission statements: we commit to all students learning at all levels.

Armando and Robinson Elementary

Armando's teacher and her multigrade, collaborative teacher team cooperatively plan upcoming teaching and learning for their kindergarten, first-, and second-grade students. While there are challenges associated with serving as the only first-grade teacher at Robinson Elementary, Ms. Hollings prefers to view the situation positively. Through her frequent collaborations with her kindergarten partner, she understands the content and instructional strategies that her students experienced last year; through the work with her second-grade partner, she appreciates the expectations for which she is preparing her students.

Armando's needs have led to fruitful, necessary conversations with her kindergarten colleague. The benefits are twofold: (1) Ms. Hollings learns of strategies from her kindergarten partner that allow her to provide phonological awareness supports to Armando that are not typically a large part of the first-grade essential standards. (2) Her kindergarten colleague learns about the gaps in reading that are impacting Armando's success, allowing her to reflect on and revise her planning and differentiation for this year's kindergarten students.

The three-member team collaborates on several topics that impact each of their classrooms.

- **Alternative phonics:** Ms. Hollings and her team have noted that synthetic phonics, the type of phonics that most basal programs employ (and that serves most students well), do not work with a small percentage of students, including Armando. Thus, her team researches and employs many types of phonics to ensure that all students crack the code, allowing them to access text closer and closer to their grade level.

- **Scaffolds for comprehension:** Each of the teachers on the K–2 collaborative team serves students who cannot access grade-level text with the accuracy and fluency that allow them to efficiently practice comprehension. *Comprehension*, making meaning of text, is the whole point of all reading instruction, and students like Armando are at risk of falling further and further behind peers in comprehension if scaffolds are not provided to ensure they can access text. Ms. Hollings provides Armando with opportunities for shared reading, guided reading, and buddy reading, and also ensures that Armando practices making meaning of text while listening to rich text at the classroom's listening center. In addition, through communications with the school's leadership team, her team has gained access to leveled texts.

- **Writing supports:** In the absence of writing supports, Armando and other students simply do not produce the quantity or quality of writing that will allow them to demonstrate their understanding of new content, and their proficiency in writing is negatively affected. Ms. Hollings assigns Armando finger-strengthening tasks that he completes as an independent activity. She also allows him to use mobile devices and computers to produce written assignments. The K–2 team uses a differentiated, word-study approach to teaching spelling, instead of the traditional and ineffective memorization of lists of words. This provides Armando and other students the opportunity to learn the patterns and morphologies of words, developing their decoding, encoding, vocabulary, and spelling skills. Finally, Ms. Hollings and her team have collaboratively developed sentence starters and frames that allow Armando and other students to approach writing with more confidence and competence.

- **Concrete mathematics supports:** Most traditional mathematics supports rely too heavily on procedural approaches to teaching and learning. Ms. Hollings and her colleagues recognize that these approaches will not work for Armando and other students, particularly when conceptual *and* procedural understanding is the goal. Whenever mathematics instruction is planned and delivered, Ms. Hollings and her colleagues incorporate concrete, representational, *and* abstract strategies to help students understand and interact with mathematics topics. In addition, Ms. Hollings and her colleagues have committed to introducing all topics using three complementary modalities: visual, auditory, and kinesthetic. Upon reflecting on their practices, they acknowledged that they too often taught through either auditory or visual means, and recognize the benefits to student learning from tapping into multiple learning modalities. Kinesthetic approaches are particularly beneficial to primary-age boys and reinforce the visual and auditory ways of presenting topics.

- **Language support:** Ms. Hollings and her colleagues each spend at least thirty minutes a day explicitly teaching the functions and forms of the English language. Students are given numerous opportunities to develop their oral and written fluency with English. Several of these fluency practices allow Armando to move and talk, which is particularly beneficial. In addition, her team continuously develops their use of SDAIE (specially designed academic instruction in English) to ensure that English learners, and all students, can successfully access instruction in all content areas. Pictorial-input charts and cognitive-content dictionaries are two of the favored and highly effective supports that her team employs. Armando accesses these supports during class to build his academic vocabulary.

- **Respect, responsibility, and readiness:** Ms. Hollings and her team define, teach, model, and reinforce social-behavioral expectations at the beginning of every day, during morning meetings, and throughout the day, particularly during transitions, such as from the classroom to recess. Armando has particular difficulty with appropriate social interactions and with working independently. While the consistent modeling and positive reinforcement that he receives (verbally and through Robinson "caught-being-good cards") have resulted in improved behaviors, he requires more frequent supports, reminders, and monitoring.

- **Motivation, perseverance, and organization:** Just as Ms. Hollings and her team define, teach, model, and reinforce social-behavioral expectations continuously, they also focus attention on the academic-behavioral expectations for students. Her team accepts that, particularly for primary-age students, they are responsible for teaching students the rules of school—the habits and strategies that successful students practice. Aside from Armando's difficulties with independence, which Ms. Hollings and her colleagues attribute more to social difficulties than deficits in self-regulation, he is motivated to learn new information, he works diligently, and he loves to have an organized table and classroom. In fact, Armando has been given the ongoing role of classroom organizer and cleaner, a task that positively impacts his social-behavioral and fine motor needs.

The core instruction that Ms. Hollings, with support from her collaborative teacher team, has provided to Armando has proven to be beneficial. Common assessments, both formal and informal, reveal that Armando is mastering most grade-level essentials. However, in the areas of reading and social behaviors, core supports are typically not enough. In these areas, additional supports are necessary to supplement Tier 1 instruction.

Katie and Wilson Elementary

Mr. Beyer, Katie's teacher, can't imagine teaching without collaborating with the other fourth-grade teachers at Wilson. The team has committed to providing all students with improved reading comprehension support. To achieve this goal, these teachers have participated in professional development in the area of close reading. The five-member team has developed a shared knowledge around the strategies associated with close reading, and staff have translated this professional learning into daily teaching and learning. Katie has a sharp, inquisitive mind, and the increasingly analytic reading activities in which the class has engaged have been motivating to her. Katie and her classmates have previously performed better at tasks that require more implicit interactions with text than with tasks that require them to explicitly recall key information. Mr. Beyer and his team's response to this need has been to place an increased emphasis on summarization within all content.

Katie also experiences difficulties with fluency, and Mr. Beyer and his colleagues have embedded daily fluency support within core reading instruction. While students' accuracy and rate could improve, the prosody or expression with which they read requires more attention. Katie, in particular, reads robotically; Mr. Beyer has been focusing on her reading with greater phrasing, and he believes that this will positively impact Katie's comprehension.

Katie's math performance is average. Mr. Beyer and the rest of the team, however, know that she is capable of more, and given the increased rigor and depth of mastery required by the CCSS, the fourth-grade team is devoting more time to supporting students in justifying their solutions to problems. Through scaffolds to support written and graphical justifications, Katie and her classmates are receiving more support through both whole-group and small-group supports. The collaborative teacher team is seeking to improve students' perseverance and expression of viable arguments.

While Katie's social behaviors are compliant, if not enthusiastically positive, Mr. Beyer and the fourth-grade teaching team are encouraging her to continue to write in her journal both to improve her writing and to help her process social-emotional challenges. Wilson Elementary promotes positive behaviors; Katie meets the school's "Respect, Make Good Decisions, Solve Your Own Problem" expectations. However, the school, Mr. Beyer included, is concerned about Katie's emotional state of being. While Katie sometimes meets the school's academic-behavioral expectations of "Strategy, Self-Efficacy, Self-Starting," her confidence and stickwithitness could improve. Consequently, Mr. Beyer has begun chunking both her short- and long-term assignments to help improve perseverance and work completion. Moreover, her self-regulatory skills—organizing her binder, keeping an agenda, taking notes—have recently become a concern. Mr. Beyer is most concerned on behalf of Katie, though, because she appears so sad and has not been receptive to requests for assistance. Katie is an avid, conscientious writer; however, her emotional state may require more intensive supports.

Holly and Roosevelt Elementary

Ms. Blackburn has tailored an instructional program to build Holly's literacy and numeracy skills. Holly also participates in a general education setting for reading and mathematics, in a class that is cotaught by Ms. O'Connor, a general education teacher, and Mrs. Banning, a special education teacher. Ms. O'Connor and Mrs. Banning collaboratively plan reading and mathematics instruction for a sixth-grade class that includes general education students, students with mild disabilities, and students with more profound disabilities. While Holly does not verbally contribute to class discussions, she completes tasks with supports, and Mrs. Banning brings classwork to Ms. Blackburn so that she and Holly can continue to engage with the sixth-grade content, with appropriate modifications.

Ms. Blackburn and Holly are currently focusing on practicing the reading skills and strategies with both literary and expository texts, as defined in next-generation standards. Ms. Blackburn provides scaffolds; Holly reads text that is within her instructional zone, and she responds using sign language that Ms. Blackburn records. Holly also uses Boardmaker to visually represent her comprehension, and she is increasingly producing writing, completing sentence starters that Ms. Blackburn has created within a word-processing program. These sentence starters have been shared with all staff at Roosevelt to support students in general and special education settings who have difficulty expressing their understanding in writing.

Holly and her classmates are full participants in Roosevelt's positive behavior system. When Holly is "caught being good"—when she demonstrates positive, responsible, integrity, dependable, or engaged (PRIDE) behaviors—any and all staff members acknowledge and recognize her positive behaviors, either verbally or with Roosevelt Tiger Tickets. (As a Tier 2 support, Holly also serves as a volunteer supervisor during the primary-grade lunches, and she distributes Tiger Tickets.)

Field trips are also part of Holly's core program. Most recently, Holly and her sixth-grade classmates have visited the local junior high school that they will attend next year. They will make several more visits to the school, navigating the offices, common spaces, and classrooms, ensuring a smooth transition when the next school year begins. Holly practices her self-sufficiency goals during these off-campus experiences.

Franklin and Middletown Middle School

For many years, Franklin's teachers and Middletown's schoolwide teams delayed providing supports since his academic skills appeared to be sound. However, they are beginning to realize that no matter how well they differentiate core expectations, some students will need some help after initial instruction, and still other students will enter their grade with significant gaps in foundational skills or severe obstacles related to effort, attendance, or behavior. Although Franklin had not been identified with Tier 3 behavioral needs in the past, his teachers were weary of his antics and believed their limited attention and resources would be better directed to students who appreciate it and appear to be gaining from it.

Mr. Huberman, Franklin's math teacher, has noticed a number of doodles on Franklin's work that involve mathematics. He has begun conversations with Franklin about some of the rules of numbers and is impressed by his raw knowledge. He asked Franklin to consider entering math competitions (Pascal, Cayley, and Fermat) and was happy that Franklin agreed. From Franklin's perspective, it was initially a chance to get out of class, but he has found the challenge interesting. Mr. Huberman plans to share this news with the rest of Franklin's teachers at their upcoming team meeting.

While he fully understands the REAL (respect, effort, attitude, leadership) acronym, Franklin has not felt compelled to also follow the expectations. He does not feel a connection to the school or its culture and believes it was created to control the behavior of students, not to create expectations for all members of the school community. He struggles with respect being expected but not delivered and believes he is demonstrating leadership, but not in the way it has been defined. To refocus his energy, Ms. Fainsilber, the student leadership coach, has asked him to be part of a group that will work with students at the neighboring elementary school on their science fair projects. Her goal is to lessen Franklin's distractibility, which she recognizes as an antecedent to more serious negative behavior. By explaining the expectations of being a role model and reviewing expectations prior to the visit to the elementary school, she has noticed a decrease in the intensity and frequency of his acting out.

Anna and Heartland High School

Though Anna's daily schedule is similar to those of other students, her academic program is significantly modified to best meet her needs. Evidence from the HHS school psychologist revealed that Anna has severe difficulties with basic numerical functions, such as addition and subtraction. In reading, Anna is still developing knowledge of phonics and is working on basic fluency and comprehension skills. Her limited vocabulary and deficient comprehension abilities make any effort at reading to learn difficult. Though Anna typically does poorly on assessments, functionally she has a strong will and excels in areas of interest to her.

Anna has flourished at HHS, and due to intensive interventions, both behavioral and academic, has become less depressed and more interactive with her peers. The school's SIT created a robust array of interventions to help address her physical and academic needs. This team, in conjunction with the course-alike collaborative teams that oversee Anna's classes, collectively decided to modify Anna's academic program to best suit her needs. Though Anna receives a modified curriculum, her teachers, support specialists, and administrators ensure that she has access to instruction in prioritized grade-level standards. Just because Anna has different learning needs does not mean she should be excluded from receiving a rigorous academic and life-skills experience.

Anna's profound disabilities, especially physical, make it unlikely that she will ever be able to fully support herself through gainful employment. Independent living is a lofty ambition for Anna and, as such, is the primary long-term goal guiding Anna's IEP. High levels of learning for Anna consist of supports that will allow her to live independent of, but supported by, her parents or care professionals.

The staffs and schools of our five students collectively accepted responsibility for all students' success. This begins with a focused, differentiated Tier 1 instructional experience for all students. We expect students to live productive lives; therefore, all students must develop the skills and attributes that allow them to live productive lives.

We can predict that some students will need more time and different approaches to learn prioritized content. Schools, then, must be ready with supplemental Tier 2 interventions for these predictable occurrences.

CHAPTER 5

Uniting Skill and Will With Supplemental Interventions

A fundamental principle of RTI at Work is timely interventions when there is evidence that students are not learning. In an RTI at Work school, the team best positioned to take the lead in providing Tier 2 academic interventions is the collaborative teacher team. This team has:

- Assumed collective responsibility for identifying and unwrapping essential standards

- Concentrated and delivered differentiated core instruction

- Crafted common formative assessments (CFAs)

- Gathered and analyzed convergent assessment information

The team should assume primary responsibility for ensuring access to extra time and support in learning essential academic content. Before describing how collaborative teacher teams can provide these supports—a little more time and alternative approaches to mastering essentials—we should further describe the tasks of the collaborative teacher teams that inform these interventions.

Targeting Interventions

In our experiences, one of the reasons why interventions fail to result in students rapidly responding with increased levels of learning is that the interventions are not sufficiently targeted. When teams have more precise information about the causes of student difficulties, they can be much more successful in remediating these difficulties.

There are relatively simple practices in which collaborative teacher teams can engage that will significantly improve their CFAs and improve the targetedness of their interventions.

Unwrapping Essential Standards

The first practice is to unwrap essential standards into learning targets. Standards are too often broadly written; mastering an essential standard requires that students know and apply more discrete skills. Therefore, we recommend that collaborative teacher teams unwrap essential standards into learning targets. This will allow for better design of CFAs. More importantly, analyses of CFAs that provide specific evidence on specific learning targets, and not less-precise data on more broadly written standards, can allow collaborative teacher teams to provide more targeted Tier 2 interventions.

Accurately Crafting CFAs

Supplemental supports will also be more effective when collaborative teacher teams craft CFAs that more accurately represent and measure student learning of essentials. The most common method of assessing student learning is through selected-response (for example, multiple-choice) tests, yet these types of tests only measure *knowledge-level* learning targets. Other types of items—such as short answer and extended response—and other types of tests will ensure that teams better assess the other three types of learning targets: *reasoning, performance*, and *product* (Stiggins, 2004). While a complete summary of designing CFAs is beyond the scope of this book, collaborative teacher teams will more accurately gather information and provide more targeted interventions with more well-designed assessments.

Accurately Analyzing CFAs

Convergent assessment of student mastery of academic essentials involves both accurate analysis of student deficits at the learning-target level *and* open, courageous conversations regarding the teaching strategies that led to the highest levels of student learning. We recommend that collaborative teacher teams be *tight* on which essential standards will be addressed in a given block of time and *tight* on what CFAs will be administered and when they will be given, but teaching pacing and strategies should be loose. This action research is a fundamental principle of PLCs and allows courageous collaborative teacher teams to compare results and identify the most successful practices among the team. For collaborative analysis, we provide a tool in *Simplifying Response to Intervention* (Buffum et al., 2012), shown in figure 5.1.

Common Assessment Team Protocol

This protocol is designed to help a teacher team quickly and efficiently discuss a common assessment. If each teacher reviews his or her own assessment data prior to the team meeting, then the team should be able to collectively complete this activity within a typical team meeting of forty-five to sixty minutes.

1. Which specific students did not demonstrate mastery on which specific standards? (Respond by the student, by the standard)

2. Which instructional practices proved to be most effective?

3. What patterns can we identify from the student mistakes?

4. How can we improve this assessment?

5. What interventions are needed to provide failed students with additional time and support?

6. How will we extend learning for students who have mastered the standard(s)?

Source: Reprinted from Buffum et al., 2012, p. 116.

Figure 5.1: Common assessment team protocol.

*Visit **go.solution-tree.com/rtiatwork** for a reproducible version of this figure.*

Among other information, this tool guides conversations of the collaborative teacher teams regarding:

- Which students have not yet mastered essential learning

- Which learning targets of essential standards, specifically, require more time and an alternative approach to learn

- Which teacher has had the greatest relative levels of success in helping students master these targets and essentials; if all teachers on the team require more guidance, they will reach out to schoolwide teams

Responding to CFAs

Another common task associated with CFAs in an RTI at Work school is the collective team response when students do not learn essentials—what we describe as Tier 2 academic intervention. This critically important aspect of RTI is described later in this chapter.

Addressing Social and Academic Behaviors

Before moving to how we can provide Tier 2 intervention, we must address social and academic behaviors. As part of Tier 1, we:

- Clearly define common, schoolwide behaviors that will be consistently accepted

- Commit to explicitly teaching and modeling the behaviors we want students to exhibit

- Identify how the behaviors we want to see will be positively reinforced as we modify behaviors and help students build better habits

We will discuss universal screening for behaviors to identify students at the greatest risk for misbehavior in the next chapter, but in this section, we will address how we can identify and diagnose the causes of misbehaviors that occur within the school year so that they do not escalate.

We must consistently apply and reinforce student behaviors and behavioral expectations in all classrooms, grade levels, and environments across campuses. Schoolwide teams must take the lead on behavior. An efficient, systematic staff recommendation process must be one part of a school's method for identifying students who are at risk, and can be particularly important when identifying students who may need behavior supports. Collecting common assessment data is an important way that schools identify students. Common assessment data in the area of academic skills come from CFAs; common assessment data in the behavioral skills can come from the consistent, frequent completion of behavior documentation forms.

The frequent, consistent gathering of information on minor misbehaviors allows us to collectively, proactively respond to student needs. When a frequency of misbehaviors occurs and a pattern emerges, teams can diagnose the causes (or antecedents or functions) of student difficulties with the Common Assessment Team Protocol from figure 5.1 (page 79).

When students are experiencing behavioral difficulties—or when misbehavior impacts academic difficulties—identifying the need early and diagnosing the causes of the misbehavior are critical to targeting supports that will help the students begin to build better habits.

We can predict that, despite our best first instruction in Tier 1, some students will need a little more time and an alternative approach or strategy to master the essentials of the course or content area. In our experience, this is the conclusion reached by nearly every collaborative teacher team at the conclusion of units of instruction when analyzing data from CFAs. Let's be ready. By building time into our instructional units and instructional days, we can ensure that teachers have time to reteach and that students are given the extended amounts of time that they will need. We call this process the Teaching-Assessing Cycle, a central element to RTI at Work.

Teams start by ensuring that time exists in which they can supplement with supports, even before they know exactly which students will require more time with exactly which essential standards and learning targets. For schools that have not yet built a thirty- to forty-five-minute intervention block into their instructional day, teams agree to set aside a day in their plan book when no new content is covered, and during which targeted reteaching can occur. This plan represents a solid start to collectively responding but is not sufficiently frequent and perhaps not possible at secondary schools in which staff teach courses during a different period of the day. Instead, schools are increasingly building an intervention block into the bell schedule. Teams can then plan and provide supplemental supports for essential standards on an almost-daily basis.

The information gleaned from collaborative teacher-team analyses of CFA data informs these supports. These analyses, and the subsequent focus of supports, can occur at the end of the unit, but teams should also work toward administering, analyzing, and collectively responding to data from mid-unit CFAs. We can very often identify students struggling to master a unit's essentials well before the unit is complete. The earlier we determine the need, the more timely and successful our response can be. Students who have not yet mastered essentials receive support at the learning-target level. Students who have already demonstrated mastery have the opportunity to engage with the essentials at greater levels of depth and complexity. Schools often choose to group students by need during these sessions. The CFA analysis process can determine the teachers chosen to address these different types of needs. Teachers who have demonstrated a greater relative level of success in helping students master specific essential standards are the best staff members to provide this support. Although collaborative teacher teams take the lead when providing these supplemental academic supports, other staff can be involved. Many schools, in the spirit of collectively accepting responsibility for all student learning, have assigned support staff to collaborative teacher teams during the intervention block, thereby allowing reduced teacher-student ratios.

Employing Behavioral Strategies

When a student exhibits a pattern of misbehavior, or when behavioral difficulties exacerbate or cause academic difficulties, we must employ behavioral strategies. The search for the perfect behavioral strategy has assumed holy grail–like status. The good news is that there are research-based behavioral strategies that we can access, learn, and employ—even though most of these strategies will appear to be common sense rather than the new, magic bullet for helping students improve their behavior that many educators hope for. Thus, we recommend that schools, led by schoolwide teams:

- Informally analyze the functions of a student's misbehavior, as described previously

- Identify a singular target behavior to improve

- Select a strategy that will help the student, and the student's teachers, improve the behavior

- Ensure that the student receives reteaching on the target behavior

- Ensure that the student and the teachers fully understand the strategy and how it will be used

- Embed the strategy within a CI/CO process

Later, we describe CI/CO and explain how it can be a powerful, transformative way to help students improve their behaviors. We'll start, however, with how collaborative teacher teams can monitor student response to the Tier 2 academic supports described earlier in the chapter.

Monitoring Progress

There is no RTI if we do not determine whether or not students are responding. We do not progress monitor because it is a state or district requirement or because school psychologists demand graphs; we progress monitor because we must support students who are at risk with a sense of urgency. Monitoring a student's progress allows us to know if we have successfully matched a supplemental support to a student's need. Monitoring progress also allows us to check on the general effectiveness of our interventions.

As previously mentioned, schools have overcomplicated the monitoring process. In fact, monitoring student response to Tier 2 academic interventions is quite simple when we recall the focus of Tier 2 supports: more time and alternative strategies to master grade-level and course-specific essential standards. Given this focus, does it not make sense to simply monitor progress using alternative versions of the same CFA that led teams to intervene in the first place?

Curriculum-based measurements (CBMs) have become popular but misunderstood and misapplied tools in RTI. We will address CBMs in more detail in the following chapter. In regard to monitoring Tier 2 progress, however, there is not a CBM for biology, pre-algebra, ancient civilizations, or comparing and contrasting. CBMs are used to sensitively monitor student gains in foundational skills, such as early phonics and computation. To monitor student response to supports designed to provide them more time and alternative strategies to master essential standards, alternate versions of CFAs are a valid option. As described earlier, CI/CO is a simple, research-based, powerful process for monitoring student progress in response to behavior supports.

After the schoolwide team has led the informal analysis of the function and causes of a student's misbehavior, identified a target behavior, and selected and supported the student and the student's teachers with a strategy to assist in improving behavior, CI/CO can be used to manage and monitor the effectiveness of the support. There are several key features of CI/CO, but the ultimate goal is for:

- The use of CI/CO to be gradually reduced
- The student to take responsibility for monitoring his or her own behaviors

Some schools view CI/CO as part monitoring and part intervention, due to its mentoring feature. Within the process, students check in and check out with staff members with whom they have a relationship and who can coach and guide them through improving their performance. Check-ins and check-outs are brief, specific, reflective pep talks that ask students to identify successes, areas for improvement, and goals. Another important feature of CI/CO is the focus of the process. We do not recommend that teams select multiple behaviors to address, at least initially. As students demonstrate progress in one behavioral area, add others while retaining the former.

The next feature of CI/CO in Tier 2 is the definition of measurable, observable traits. This allows both the students and teachers to more accurately assess performance. Significantly, both the students and teachers assess; we recommend that students first evaluate their performance, followed by a quick assessment by the teacher. Teachers need not provide debriefs or critiques; that's the job of the CI/CO mentor. Teachers feel overwhelmed and the process is difficult to sustain when they must provide debriefs at the conclusion of lessons.

The frequency of monitoring within the day can vary based on student age and the severity of need. At the conclusion of the day, the mentor totals the points and reflects on successes and challenges, including determining whether the student reached the target number of points.

CI/CO works, but the process must be completed consistently, positively, and in the spirit of collective responsibility. It should be adjusted as students succeed or when more, or different, supports are determined to be necessary. The process produces data that can reveal progress to students and staff. It places responsibilities on students to assess and monitor their own progress as they build better habits. It allows schools to be proactive in helping to improve student behavior.

Armando and Robinson Elementary

Ms. Hollings and her kindergarten and grade 2 collaborative teacher-team partners have aligned their daily schedules so that for four days a week, they share a thirty-minute intervention and enrichment block during which students can receive differentiated supports. While the grade-level essentials that they have identified and unwrapped are specific to their grade levels, they have aligned the timing of their units and the dates on which they administer common assessments. This allows them to support one another in the analysis of results and to have similarly timely information to which they can collectively respond within the intervention and enrichment block. Ms. Hollings and her partners completed one other task when cognitively planning that enriched their instruction and allowed for more collective intervention and enrichment; to the extent possible, they aligned the concepts that they were addressing within major content areas—phonological awareness, phonics, comprehension, mathematics—so that, while the essential standards and learning targets are distinct, the enduring understandings are common. This ongoing process is not as challenging as they suspected it might be; kindergarten, first grade, and second grade share important outcomes.

An important part of the team's analysis of CFA data is determining which students need which supports, and which team member will provide them. The Robinson Elementary leadership team has assigned a special education paraprofessional to support the members of the K–2 collaborative teacher team during their intervention and enrichment block. The paraprofessional participates in collaborative conversations with the team when the teachers are designing their use of this time. The paraprofessional guides the work of one of the enrichment groups; students have been prepared to work collaboratively on rich tasks and, to the extent possible, to direct their own learning during these sessions.

Analyses of data often reveal that Armando requires more time and an alternative approach to master essential standards. The team provides support in reading on Mondays and Thursdays, and in mathematics on Tuesdays and Fridays. (Wednesday is an early-dismissal day for students so that teachers have time to collaborate, so the team has not scheduled the intervention and enrichment block.) The alternative approaches required for Armando to master reading essentials often involve his inability to decode grade-level text. Ms. Hollings and the kindergarten teacher, Mr. Stahl, provide supplemental core phonics instruction with supports that follow Orton-Gillingham guidelines: less dependent on the discrimination and blending of specific phonemes, and based more on word parts (Ritchey & Goeke, 2006). While these supports seem to be preventing Armando from falling further behind, they are not closing the gap; Armando is not yet decoding like a first grader.

Armando's team is very conscious of his comprehension needs as well. His teachers understand that phonics is just the means to the end, and that the sole purpose of all reading instruction is comprehension. They worry that by focusing so much time on decoding, Armando's comprehension abilities do not receive the attention they require. Therefore, the team focuses on providing Armando with opportunities to practice high-leverage strategies with text that he can readily access, which typically means primer texts that are not found in most first-grade anthologies. The high-leverage strategies on which the team focuses its supports include summarization, compare-contrast, and visualization. Focusing on mastery of these comprehension skills during supplemental supports, instead of on reteaching the dozens of skills and strategies present in the first-grade reading program, is equipping Armando with effective skills that he can independently employ—assuming he can decode the text. Armando's comprehension with supports is sound; his decoding and phonics abilities continue to worry the team.

During intervention and enrichment time for mathematics, Ms. Hollings and her team focus on number sense and numeracy. The extra time and alternative strategies that Armando needs to master first-grade essentials typically relate to difficulties with correspondence, conservation, and cardinality. Difficulties with these basic numeracy skills impact Armando's knowledge of place value, which impacts his ability to understand decomposing numbers, which in turn impacts his abilities to add and subtract numbers. Thus, Tier 2 supports for Armando in mathematics center on concrete practice with numeracy.

While Armando's academic needs seem to be greater than his behavioral needs, Armando does require more frequent and specific supports with respect, responsibility, and readiness. With the guidance of the Robinson Elementary leadership team, Ms. Hollings and her colleagues conducted a simplified analysis of the function of Armando's behavior. They determined that most of his misbehavior occurs during reading and when he is engaged in free play, both inside and outside the classroom. During reading tasks, Armando's misbehaviors seem to be motivated by his desire to avoid the tasks. To address this cause, Armando has learned strategies for seeking assistance, and his team has adopted specific strategies to ensure that tasks are within Armando's zone of proximal development and that the directions are clear. During free play, Armando's misbehavior seems to be attention seeking in nature; he does not know how to initiate play, and his attempts are not well received by classmates, resulting in his acting out. To address these behaviors, the school counselor taught Armando strategies for joining groups and for reading social cues. The counselor also taught Armando's teacher team these strategies and gave the teachers simple reminders that they can share. Ms. Hollings has experienced success using precorrections with Armando; before reading tasks and before free play, she reminds Armando of his strategies by quietly placing precorrection cards on his desk. Armando's CI/CO mentor is Mr. Stahl, his kindergarten teacher, with whom he still has a close bond. He manages and monitors the effectiveness of these behavior supports using the CI/CO process—the same procedure used across the school.

Armando's team is proud that he is a motivated and cooperative young learner. The teachers feel that the Tier 2 supports that they are providing in the areas of comprehension, mathematics, and social behaviors are resulting in an adequate response, and they anticipate that, with continued support in first grade, he will steadily close gaps in these areas. They remain concerned, however, in the area of phonics. Armando is not making the progress that they expect and that he needs to make to independently access the increasingly complex narrative and expository texts that primary students are encountering. The K–2 team has reached out to the schoolwide leadership and intervention team to further determine the types of supports that will result in greater levels of success. Figure 5.2 and figure 5.3 (page 88) are examples of Armando's completed pro-solve process and subsequent monitoring plan data for Tiers 1 and 2.

Student: _____Armando_____   **Meeting Date:** _____October 1_____

Participants: Ms. Hollings (first grade), Mr. Stahl (kindergarten), Ms. Walker (second grade), Mrs. Curso (counselor)

	Targeted Outcomes	1. Concern	2. Cause	3. Desired Outcomes	4. Intervention Steps	5. Who Takes Responsibility
Led by Teacher Teams	Grade-level essential standards	Simple phonics	Deficits in phonological awareness?	Ability to decode first-grade text accurately, with the appropriate rate and the appropriate expression	Additional small-group practice with manipulating phonemes and practice segmenting and blending sound using Elkonin-type activities	Kindergarten and first-grade teacher
	Immediate prerequisite skills	Phonemic awareness	Auditory processing?	Ability to hear and process sounds to decode text	Additional small-group practice with manipulating phonemes	Kindergarten and first-grade teacher
	English language	Proper forms to express functional language	Emerging English language proficiency	Consistent use of the proper grammatical forms	Scaffolds with Tier 1, such as sentence frames	First-grade teacher
Led by Schoolwide Teams	Academic behaviors					
	Social behaviors	Inability to work independently and difficulty connecting with peers	Lack of self-regulatory skills	Ability to work independently on differentiated tasks and collaborate and play with others without conflicts	Self-selected time-outs during class and steps for initiating play	Teachers and counselor
	Health and home					

Next Meeting Date: _____October 30_____

Figure 5.2: Armando's pro-solve Tier 1 and 2 targeting process.

Student: _____ Armando _____   **Meeting Date:** _____ October 15

Participants: Ms. Hollings (first grade), Mr. Stahl (kindergarten), Ms. Walker (second grade), Mrs. Curso (counselor)

	Targeted Outcomes	Desired Outcomes	Interventions and Action Steps	Who	Data Point 1	Data Point 2	Data Point 3	Data Point 4	Data Point 5
Led by Teacher Teams	Essential standards	Ability to decode first-grade text accurately, with the appropriate rate and the appropriate expression	Additional small-group practice with manipulating phonemes and practice segmenting and blending sound using Elkonin-type activities	Kindergarten and first-grade teacher	DIBELS PSF (12) DIBELS NWF-WWR (2)	DIBELS PSF (13) DIBELS NWF-WWR (2)	DIBELS PSF (12) DIBELS NWF-WWR (2)		
	Immediate prerequisite skills	Ability to hear and process sounds to decode text	Additional small-group practice with manipulating phonemes	Kindergarten and first-grade teacher	DIBELS FSF (8) DIBELS LNF (16)	DIBELS FSF (10) DIBELS LNF (23)	DIBELS FSF (11) DIBELS LNF (34)		
	English language	Consistent use of the proper grammatical forms	Scaffolds with Tier 1, such as sentence frames	First-grade teacher	Consistency of grammatically correct oral language (2 out of 4)	Consistency of grammatically correct oral language (3 out of 4)	Consistency of grammatically correct oral language (3 out of 4)		
Led by Schoolwide Teams	Academic behaviors								
	Social behaviors	Ability to work independently on differentiated tasks and collaborate and play with others without conflicts	Self-selected time-outs during class and steps for initiating play	Kindergarten teacher	CI/CO (average of 12 daily points/week)	CI/CO (average of 15 daily points/week)	CI/CO (average of 20 daily points/week)		
	Health and home								

Next Meeting Date: _____ October 29

Figure 5.3: Armando's pro-solve Tier 1 and 2 monitoring plan.

Katie and Wilson Elementary

Katie's social-emotional needs are a frequent topic of conversation among her teachers: Mr. Beyer and his four colleagues on the fourth-grade team. Ms. Hendricks, in particular, has taken an interest in Katie. Although Katie still seems reluctant to allow herself to get close to any staff member, Ms. Hendricks has redoubled her efforts at making a connection. Katie checks in with Ms. Hendricks each morning and checks out with her every afternoon. Wilson Elementary has established weekly areas of focus to reinforce its schoolwide behavioral goals. When the week's goal is related to a strategy, such as note taking, Ms. Hendricks spends time with Katie looking through her binder for examples of note taking. Ms. Hendricks provides supplemental Tier 2 support in this critical strategy by modeling taking notes on her plans for the upcoming weekend with her niece, who will be visiting from out of town. Katie receives extra attention on the strategy through a unique context, and through sharing a little about herself, Ms. Hendricks tries to build some trust with Katie.

Mr. Beyer and the fourth-grade team design and deliver Tier 2 supports during a daily thirty-minute flex period; they are joined during this period by the school's two special education teachers, thereby allowing the team to divide the five classrooms of fourth graders among seven staff members. With space at a premium, the two special education teachers provide Tier 2 supports to groups of students within two of the fourth-grade classrooms. Three days a week, the team provides more time and alternative strategies to the essentials of fourth-grade reading. During these sessions, Katie receives support in comprehension, advanced phonics, and fluency. While fluency is a part of the team's core instruction, Katie's self-corrections and frequent repetitions of words and phrases negatively impact the fluidity with which she reads, and impact her comprehension. The Tier 2 fluency interventions she receives involve practice with chunking and phrasing, repeatedly reading short text at her independent level. She also has difficulty when the essential comprehension skills and strategies that Mr. Beyer teaches are presented abstractly. While Mr. Beyer is using more concrete representations of comprehension, such as graphic organizers, Katie is benefiting from more time and practice with this nonlinguistic representation of comprehension strategies. Katie's mathematical reasoning is sound; her success is often hampered by her lack of computational fluency. As part of the two-day-a-week Tier 2 supports in the essentials of the mathematics unit, Katie also receives direct support in attaining greater mastery of facts. The team shares multiple strategies for making sense of facts, including reinforcing the commutative property with addition and multiplication, and using addition to drive subtraction and multiplication to drive division. The team is also providing support in decomposing numbers to allow Katie and a few other classmates greater success with multidigit computation. While the team's collective analyses of common assessment data often reveal that Katie would benefit from more time and alternative approaches to master Tier 1 essentials, she is currently responding adequately to Tier 1 and 2 academic supports.

Katie still appears sad and withdrawn. In addition to the support of Ms. Hendricks, the Wilson Elementary schoolwide leadership team has become involved. The school principal has asked Mrs. Martin, a district counselor, to check on Katie in the classroom every week. The principal reached out to Mrs. Martin after Mr. Beyer and the team noted Katie's self-injurious behaviors, which only confirmed their concerns about her social-emotional state. Mrs. Martin has been careful to avoid singling Katie out; instead, she interacts with many students in Mr. Beyer's class. She is observant of Katie's behaviors in class, however, and makes notes each day before leaving campus. She shares these weekly notes with Wilson's leadership team, providing them with an emerging profile of Katie. Katie does not make eye contact with others and will only speak to peers or adults when directly asked a question, and even then her responses are monosyllabic and brief. She completes independent tasks diligently, although she rushes through her work. She is much less successful when working in a group. She does not initiate conversation and distances herself from classmates, even when working around the same table. While she attracts little attention to herself and is reasonably well liked, Mrs. Martin and other team members have noticed students beginning to snicker at Katie's clothing choices and personal grooming. The reteaching, CI/CO support, and visits from Mrs. Martin have allowed the team to gather information about Katie's strengths and needs, but the supports have not resulted in improved behaviors or a more positive attitude. Katie's mom continues to report the same concerns about Katie at home, and Mrs. Martin has provided guidance and referred Katie to a counselor in the community. Mr. Beyer, the fourth-grade team, the leadership team, and Mrs. Martin feel that more intensive supports may be necessary. Figure 5.4 and figure 5.5 (page 92) are examples of Katie's completed pro-solve process and subsequent monitoring plan data for Tiers 1 and 2.

Holly and Roosevelt Elementary

Holly's core curriculum includes explicit instruction in sign language and in reading (or signing) words by sight. Occasionally, Ms. Blackburn provides Tier 2 supports in reading comprehension to supplement the instruction Holly receives for reading in Ms. O'Connor and Mrs. Banning's cotaught class. These supports include practice with text that is within Holly's zone of proximal development, a zone that is impacted by her knowledge of written words, the vast majority of which she has learned by sight. Holly's comprehension of text, whether text through which she is guided orally that is close to the sixth-grade level or text

Student: _____ Katie _____   **Meeting Date:** _____ October 1

Participants: _ Mr. Beyer (fourth grade), Ms. Hendricks (fourth grade), Mrs. Crist (fourth grade), Mrs. McKeown (fourth grade), Ms. Wilson (fourth grade), Mrs. Cook (fourth grade), Mrs. Martin (district counselor), Ms. Mariner (social worker)

	Targeted Outcomes	**1. Concern**	**2. Cause**	**3. Desired Outcomes**	**4. Intervention Steps**	**5. Who Takes Responsibility**
Led by Teacher Teams	Grade-level essential standards	Poor fluency	Deficits in scooping and checking (reading text with rhythm)	Reading 120 words correct per minute accurately with expression	Practice scooping and chunking and phrasing at Katie's instructional level	Fourth-grade teacher
	Immediate prerequisite skills	Advanced phonics	Deficits in syllabication and morphology	Ability to decode and make meaning of all words	Additional small-group practice with identifying and blending the six syllable types, as well as affixes and roots	Fourth-grade team
	English language					
Led by Schoolwide Teams	Academic behaviors	Withdrawn, and seemingly unmotivated	Father deployed frequently	Self-regulated and self-motivated learner	Mentoring sessions with Ms. Hendricks	Ms. Hendricks
	Social behaviors					
	Health and home	Social-emotional responses to dad's deployment	Father deployed frequently	Positive outlook on life	Support of district counselor	Mrs. Martin

Next Meeting Date: _____ October 30

Figure 5.4: Katie's pro-solve Tier 1 and 2 targeting process.

Student: _____ Katie _____   **Meeting Date:** _____ October 15 _____

Participants: Mr. Beyer (fourth grade), Ms. Hendricks (fourth grade), Mrs. Crist (fourth grade), Mrs. McKeown (fourth grade), Ms. Wilson (fourth grade), Mrs. Cook (fourth grade), Mrs. Martin (district counselor), Ms. Mariner (social worker)

	Targeted Outcomes	Desired Outcomes	Interventions and Action Steps	Who	Data Point 1	Data Point 2	Data Point 3	Data Point 4	Data Point 5
Led by Teacher Teams	Essential standards	Reading 120 words correct per minute accurately with expression	Practice scooping and chunking and phrasing at Katie's instructional level	Fourth-grade teacher	DIBELS ORF (grade 4) (60 wcpm, 82% accuracy, self-corrections and repeats)	DIBELS ORF (grade 4) (66 wcpm, 80% accuracy, self-corrections and repeats)	DIBELS ORF (grade 4) (62 wcpm, 84% accuracy, self-corrections and repeats)		
	Immediate prerequisite skills	Ability to decode and make meaning of all words	Additional small-group practice with identifying and blending the six syllable types, as well as affixes and roots	Fourth-grade team	DIBELS ORF (grade 3) (75 wcpm, 87% accuracy, self-corrections and repeats)	DIBELS ORF (grade 3) (82 wcpm, 90% accuracy, self-corrections)	DIBELS ORF (grade 3) (90 wcpm, 93% accuracy, self-corrections)		
	English language								
Led by Schoolwide Teams	Academic behaviors	Self-regulated and self-motivated learner	Mentoring sessions with Ms. Hendricks	Ms. Hendricks	CI/CO (average of 12 daily points/week)	CI/CO (average of 15 daily points/week)	CI/CO (average of 20 daily points/week)		
	Social behaviors								
	Health and home	Positive outlook on life	Support of district counselor	Mrs. Martin	Surveys completed by teachers, parent, and student (21-point scale, 14-point average, high risk)	Surveys completed by teachers, parent, and student (21-point scale, 15-point average, high risk)	Surveys completed by teachers, parent, and student (21-point scale, 15-point average, high risk)		

Next Meeting Date: _____ October 29 _____

Figure 5.5: Katie's Tier 1 and 2 pro-solve monitoring plan.

that she reads independently, is improving. Ms. Blackburn focuses the majority of her Tier 2 comprehension supports on assisting Holly's meaning making through summarization and comparing and contrasting, two of the highest-yield comprehension skills. Holly uses a flow map to represent her summaries and a modified Venn diagram to represent comparing and contrasting, accessing templates within Boardmaker and a word-processing program. Ms. Blackburn's Tier 2 supports in comprehension are not only provided to students with profound disabilities like Holly; through her collaboration with fifth- and sixth-grade teachers, the team has found that students with more mild disabilities and without diagnosed disabilities also benefit from these types of approaches.

Holly occasionally requires reteaching and redirection in consistently displaying Roosevelt's positive, responsible, integrity, dependable, or engaged (PRIDE) behaviors. She responds well to pictorial redirections using precorrection or correction cards; the positive reinforcements that she receives in the general education settings and during lunches and passing periods have proven to be adequate sets of supports. In fact, the team has weaned Holly off full CI/CO progress-monitoring. While Holly still checks in and checks out every day with Mrs. Banning (who is also proficient in sign), staff do not complete the CI/CO at the conclusion of each period. Instead, staff simply prompt Holly to reflect and rate her own behavior. The team's goal is for Holly to increasingly and more accurately self-monitor.

Holly's transition to the junior high school next year has intensified the team's emphasis on practicing self-sufficiency and self-advocacy. As a supplemental set of supports in these areas, Ms. Blackburn presents Holly with pretend challenges. Holly has been taught to utilize task-completion checklists during these challenges, and she is encouraged and acknowledged for seeking supports from adults she does not know. While different situations and environments still create a bit of anxiety, Holly is responding more successfully and independently. In fact, the team has modified the task-completion checklist as an executive functioning tool for use with all students with difficulties in the area of academic behaviors. Figure 5.6 (page 94) and figure 5.7 (page 95) are examples of Holly's completed pro-solve process and subsequent monitoring plan data for Tiers 1 and 2.

Franklin and Middletown Middle School

Despite possessing the basic prerequisite skills, Franklin's behavior over his time in school has led to him missing instruction. As he has transitioned to secondary school curriculum, these gaps have accumulated. His removal from class, an almost daily occurrence, results in fifteen to twenty minutes of lost instruction; prior to and after his removal, little of academic substance is occurring,

Student: Holly   **Meeting Date:**   October 1

Participants: Ms. Blackburn (special education teacher), Ms. O'Connor (general education teacher), Mrs. Banning (special education teacher), Ms. Breo (principal)

Targeted Outcomes	1. Concern	2. Cause	3. Desired Outcomes	4. Intervention Steps	5. Who Takes Responsibility
Led by Teacher Teams					
Grade-level essential standards	Comprehension	Difficulties monitoring reading	Make meaning of text (approaching sixth-grade level) during guided reading environments	Summarization strategies at the end of sentences, paragraphs, sections, and pages	All teachers
Immediate prerequisite skills	Decoding	Nonverbal	Read an increasing number of words by sight	Repeated reading of text at independent or low instructional level	Ms. Blackburn
English language					
Led by Schoolwide Teams					
Academic behaviors	Significant difficulties with executive functioning	Communicative difficulties attributable to autism	Effective organization; Efficient life management (binder, backpack); Improved self-advocacy	Task-completion checklists	All staff
Social behaviors	Outbursts when faced with new situations	Social anxieties attributable to autism	Self-monitoring and self-regulating of behaviors	Tiger Tickets; Serving as a volunteer supervisor; Pictorial precorrection and correction cards	All staff
Health and home					

Next Meeting Date: October 15

Figure 5.6: Holly's pro-solve Tier 1 and 2 targeting process.

Student: ___Holly___   **Meeting Date:** ___October 15___

Participants: Ms. Blackburn (special education teacher), Ms. O'Connor (general education teacher), Mrs. Banning (special education teacher), Ms. Breo (principal)

	Targeted Outcomes	Desired Outcomes	Interventions and Action Steps	Who	Data Point 1	Data Point 2	Data Point 3	Data Point 4	Data Point 5
Led by Teacher Teams	Essential standards	Make meaning of text (approaching sixth-grade level) during guided reading environments	Summarization strategies at the end of sentences, paragraphs, sections, and pages	All teachers	QRI (grade 2), instructional with accuracy, frustration level with comprehension	QRI (grade 2), instructional with accuracy, frustration level with comprehension	QRI (grade 2), instructional with accuracy, frustration level with comprehension		
	Immediate prerequisite skills	Read an increasing number of words by sight	Repeated reading of text at independent or low instructional level	Ms. Blackburn	Dolch Sight Words (grade 3)—25 wcpm	Dolch Sight Words (grade 3)—27 wcpm	Dolch Sight Words (grade 3)—26 wcpm		
	English language								
Led by Schoolwide Teams	Academic behaviors	Effective organization Efficient life management (binder, backpack) Improved self-advocacy	Task-completion checklists	All staff	CI/CO (goal of self-advocacy) (average of 7 daily points/week)	CI/CO (goal of self-advocacy) (average of 8 daily points/week)	CI/CO (goal of self-advocacy) (average of 10 daily points/week)		
	Social behaviors	Self-monitoring and self-regulating of behaviors	Tiger Tickets Serving as a volunteer supervisor Pictorial precorrection and correction cards	All staff	CI/CO (goal of self-control) (average of 10 daily points/week)	CI/CO (goal of self-control) (average of 11 daily points/week)	CI/CO (goal of self-control) (average of 10 daily points/week)		
	Health and home								

Next Meeting Date: ___October 30___

Figure 5.7: Holly's pro-solve Tier 1 and 2 monitoring plan.

and the minutes have added up to significant learning loss. His teachers are noticing that, while comprehending concepts generally, his increasing lack of skills prevents him from completing tasks in a timely fashion, an antecedent to his inappropriate behaviors. Franklin's overall approach to his work at school is one of apathy. He appears bored with lessons and does not indicate a preference for any content area. In general, this apathy inhibits his engagement in work and distracts his peers. This has also led to academic penalties that, rather than creating positive change, have served to strengthen his negative social behaviors.

The members of Franklin's collaborative teacher team know it is their collective responsibility to provide the interventions required during their class time with Franklin. As tempting as it appears to remove him from class, they have recognized that this has exacerbated his struggles. Rather than pulling him from essential core instruction to provide remediation of the basic skills, they recognize he needs core instruction *and* remediation. They do not want his Tier 2 intervention to replace his access to their universal, Tier 1 core instruction. They have embarked on an approach that involves peer-to-peer instruction, targeted review time during the last ten minutes of instructional time (other students are engaged in enrichment activities where they go deeper with the intended content), and periodic ticket-out-the-door checks on how Franklin is progressing with the intended curriculum. His responses are used to monitor his progress and adjust instruction for the next class.

The team teachers have realized that they, individually and collectively, need to take responsibility for motivating Franklin. They know the importance of language and are gaining awareness of the impact that verbal comments and nonverbal body language have on Franklin's motivation level. They know in previous years at school Franklin was labeled as noncompliant, and they suspect he now is living up (or down, rather) to that label. The team has committed to fostering a supportive environment and developing a rapport with Franklin that includes using encouraging words and a positive tone of voice.

At Tier 2, they want to respond to Franklin's apathy for learning by having him set short-term goals for individual tasks and assignments. They have begun engaging him in envisioning his future and what he must do to place himself in that future. They revisit that reference point often throughout lessons. They want to help Franklin visualize a valuable real-world payoff for learning the material, as they suspect his struggles may also be attributed to his negative reaction to traditional lecture formats. They believe he will show higher rates of engagement when interacting with peers and when the connections to "future Franklin" are clear. They also know they must explicitly teach techniques for self-discipline, and they have assigned Franklin schoolwide jobs.

Finally, the team has begun giving Franklin and all other students opportunities for choice. Allowing choice in instructional activities has boosted Franklin's attention span and increased his engagement. This has been a major discussion point for the team; there had been trepidation in the past. Teachers have agreed to make a list of choice options that they are comfortable offering during typical learning activities. They also allow Franklin to take short, timed breaks during a work period and to choose when to take them.

The team is also trying to discern if Franklin's poor behavior preceded his academic struggles or vice versa. Regardless of the reasons, they know his opportunities for success are getting more limited and that this grade is a crucial time for him to turn things around. They are aware that over a third of all dropouts happen in the ninth grade and that those who repeat ninth grade have a graduation rate of only 15 percent. They have initiated a modified CI/CO form to help focus Franklin's and the staff's attention on specific, measurable behaviors that can be modified. They want to take advantage of his academic capacity and have invited him to suggest two of the categories that will appear on the document, while the team adds a category for his preparedness for work (part of the school's effort expectation) and for his work with peers (part of the school's attitude expectation).

Franklin's collaborative teacher team believes that these Tier 2 interventions in the classroom are starting to pay off. While not yet eradicating his social misbehaviors, they are confident that they have lessened the severity of those misbehaviors and are feeling like they also hold the key to affecting positive change in that regard.

Figure (page 98) 5.8 and figure 5.9 (page 99) are examples of Franklin's completed pro-solve process and subsequent monitoring plan data for Tiers 1 and 2.

Anna and Heartland High School

Because of Anna's independent living goal, her teams pay special attention to creating short-term goals that will build up to her eventual transition out of school and into the community. Anna has access to more time and differentiated supports to master the essential learning outcomes that the school teams have established. To support this goal for Anna and other students, time has become a variable at HHS: learning is a constant, and the staff assume collective responsibility for making learning for all an inevitability. As such, Anna will be allowed to stay at HHS until age twenty-one. In addition, to provide consistency in intervention, a summer academic remediation and outing program was created for Anna and several other students to assist them in attaining basic academic and life skills.

Once Anna entered HHS, she began meeting with a speech pathologist three times weekly immediately after school. By meeting after school, Anna can fully participate

Student: ___Franklin___   **Meeting Date:** ___September 20___

Participants: ___Mr. Huberman (math teacher), Ms. Fainsilber (ELA/leadership coach), Mr. Springer (counselor)___

	Targeted Outcomes	1. Concern	2. Cause	3. Desired Outcomes	4. Intervention Steps	5. Who Takes Responsibility
Led by Teacher Teams	Grade-level essential standards	Learning gaps in foundational ELA skills	Loss of instructional time	Consistent use of the proper grammatical forms and writing conventions	Additional, individualized time with teacher and with high-interest material	Ms. Fainsilber
	Immediate prerequisite skills					
	English language					
Led by Schoolwide Teams	Academic behaviors	Organization as it relates to work completion	Disengagement and lack of challenge	Completing tasks in a timely fashion and proficiently

Staying focused during housekeeping items and transition time | Organizational skills practice and executive functioning

Attention breaks | Teachers and counselor |
| | Social behaviors | | | | | |
| | Health and home | | | | | |

Next Meeting Date: ___September 27___

Figure 5.8: Franklin's pro-solve Tier 1 and 2 targeting process.

Student: Franklin   **Meeting Date:**   October 4

Participants: Mr. Huberman (math teacher), Ms. Fainsilber (ELA/leadership coach), Mr. Springer (counselor)

	Targeted Outcomes	Desired Outcomes	Interventions and Action Steps	Who	Data Point 1	Data Point 2	Data Point 3	Data Point 4	Data Point 5
Led by Teacher Teams	Essential standards	Consistent use of the proper grammatical forms and writing conventions	Additional, individualized time with teacher and with high-interest material	Ms. Fainsilber	aimsweb and chart progress	aimsweb and chart progress	aimsweb and chart progress		
	Immediate prerequisite skills								
	English language								
Led by Schoolwide Teams	Academic behaviors	Completing tasks in a timely fashion and proficiently Staying focused during house-keeping items and transition time	Organizational skills practice and executive functioning Attention breaks	Mr. Springer Ms. Fainsilber Mr. Huberman	Charting on-time task completion (baseline set at 75%) Establishing baseline for number of breaks	Part of CI/CO with social behaviors Setting goals based on reducing number and reason for breaks			
	Social behaviors								
	Health and home								

Next Meeting Date: October 11

Figure 5.9: Franklin's pro-solve Tier 1 and 2 monitoring plan.

in the individualized program HHS has set up for her during the school day. The speech pathologist had clearly defined goals based on initial assessments that monitored her articulation and expressive language on a weekly basis. Her speech pathologist conducted sessions in small groups and focused on team building, camaraderie, and social language skills development among the group—not just speech. This was extremely helpful for Anna as it assisted her in building peer relationships as well as improving her speech. This became one of several "connection points" for Anna to address her social awkwardness.

Anna's speech pathologist was nimble in her interventions, providing instruction in six-week durations. Her progress was monitored weekly, and interventions that failed to produce significant results were jettisoned, and new interventions took their place. In this environment, Anna thrived in her speech-improvement efforts. Her parents remarked that Anna had become quite a "chatter bug" due to her speech interventions. These supports have been complemented by her parents, as they have been encouraging the use of a cell phone and Skype to connect with her friends from speech class. Use of these technologies aids not only her speech and social interactions, but also helps improve skills that will be essential if she is to realize her goal of independent living.

While the school does not maintain a full-time occupational therapist on staff to support Anna's physical impairments, an itinerant OT assessed Anna's needs, designed a program for her, and then trained an HHS aide in how to deliver her program. The therapist returns monthly to test Anna's progress, refine her program, and retrain staff as needed. Anna's parents were also involved in the monthly assessments by the therapist so they could work on Anna's impairments at home as well.

Anna's regular classes are a mix of self-contained and elective courses. The electives include a focus on academic and life skills that will assist her in independent living, physical wellness, and social interactions. In her self-contained classes, Anna works with other cognitively disabled peers, a dynamic that Anna describes as "awesome" as it has provided another connection point between her and other like-abled students. Anna's teachers clearly define measurable learning goals for her and determine a timeline in which she should meet these goals. When it becomes apparent through classroom measures of progress that Anna is not responding to classroom instruction, the SIT and collaborative teams implement different strategies to ensure that she will meet learning goals.

HHS believes that all inclusion classes should be beneficial for both general and special education students alike. That is certainly the case in Anna's elective courses. Her semester-long courses include a sports management course in which regular education students train special education students for the state Special Olympics and a veterinary medicine class that exposes students to the intricacies of veterinary medicine. A coteacher or aide supports both classes, and the veterinary medicine class has a modified curriculum that focuses Anna's attention on animal care basics, an area that could benefit Anna in her post–high school occupational goal of working as a professional dog walker. Each of Anna's classes has measurable goals that are monitored and assessed using formative and summative assessments that parallel those learning standards outlined for general education students.

The rest of Anna's schedule includes self-contained, intensive yet functional reading and math instruction coupled with transition life-skills instruction. Anna's reading and math instruction are built upon research-based programs purchased by HHS for significantly struggling readers. Instruction with these programs is given in intensive one-on-one or small-group instruction sessions, multiple times each week. Because of Anna's love for technology, Anna's reading progress is monitored weekly through use of an online reading-monitoring program. If, after several weeks of intervention, assessment data indicate Anna is failing to make progress, her program strategies are changed.

Anna's parents assist the school's instructional efforts by reading at home with her on topics related to life skills, such as riding mass transit, independent living, and personal safety and care. For math, Anna's parents have supplemented the school's efforts by providing her with a bank card with a set amount of money available weekly to help her begin to manage her personal finances.

Anna's classes also work on collaboration and interpersonal relationship skills as part of life-skills planning. One particular event that Anna loves is when her class travels each month, via city bus, to participate in therapeutic riding sessions at a local horse-riding stable. Outings to the stable are paid for by a local charity organization and are planned and led by students, which requires them to count bus fares, read transit maps, and tell time schedules. Once at the stable, students are asked to follow directions on animal care, saddling, and riding the horses. Because working with animals is an area in which Anna excels, she has emerged as an academic and peer leader among her classmates, a role she relishes. Figure 5.10 (pages 102-103) and figure 5.11 (pages 104-105) are examples of Anna's completed pro-solve process and subsequent monitoring plan data for Tiers 1 and 2.

Tier 3 supports are necessary to catch students up—to fill the gap in foundational skills that inhibits students' abilities to access core content. In the absence of the Tier 2 supports described in this chapter, more time and alternative strategies to master essential core content, students may take one step forward, as a result of Tier 3 supports, but simultaneously take one step back, due to a lack of Tier 2 supports.

We can predict that, despite the best efforts of teachers and teams, some students will require more than Tier 1 and Tier 2 supports to make adequate progress to be on track to graduate ready for college, a skilled career, or in the case of students with profound disabilities, an optimally independent life. Therefore, schools must prepare with the processes and structures that will provide intensive Tier 3 supports for students with significant deficits in foundational prerequisite skills. Tier 3 is the focus of the next chapter.

Student: ___Anna___   **Meeting Date:** ___September 6___

Participants: Ms. Meganski (special education teacher), Ms. Bailey (speech pathologist), Ms. Nicholson (special education aide), Mr. Markus (Avenues teacher/advisor), Ms. Lucas (high school counselor), Ms. Gengler (special education teacher)

Led by Teacher Teams	Targeted Outcomes	1. Concern	2. Cause	3. Desired Outcomes	4. Intervention Steps	5. Who Takes Responsibility
	Grade-level essential standards	Low life-skills-related mathematical functioning	Poor adding and subtracting skills, especially in conjunction with word problems and decimal places	Make correct change with 100% accuracy	Daily use of a purchase scenario question in math class

Emphasis of this skill in speech sessions 3 times weekly | Ms. Meganski (self-contained math teacher)

Ms. Bailey (speech pathologist) |
| | Immediate prerequisite skills | Basic adding and subtracting up to 100 | Difficulty manipulating digits mentally | Be able to add and subtract numbers up to 100 without the use of manipulatives | Daily guided practice (20 minutes with aide)

Daily self-directed math practice using mental math software | Ms. Nicholson (aide) |
| | English language | | | | | |

	Targeted Outcomes	1. Concern	2. Cause	3. Desired Outcomes	4. Intervention Steps	5. Who Takes Responsibility
Led by Schoolwide Teams	Academic behaviors	Test shy or test fatigue with low effort on large assessments	Excessive large-scale measures that are perceived as low stakes by Anna	Assessment independence so Anna is not reliant on certain people for accurate assessment data	Proctor coaching from trusted adult mentors	Ms. Nicholson (aide with strongest relationship)
	Social behaviors	Socially awkward, self-conscious, with difficulty communicating in new situations	Self-consciousness due to physical disabilities	Initiates peer or community interactions for personal and life-skills purposes	Creation and mastery of three connection strategies Creation and rehearsal of an emergency plan for incontinence issues	Ms. Lucas (counselor) creates/rehearses plan with Anna privately Mr. Markus (Avenues/advisory teacher) and Ms. Gengler (special education teacher) will monitor progress of connections. Anna should attempt a peer connection daily.
	Health and home	General low muscle tone, strength, and balance; no falls, no accidents, 100% of the time	Physical disabilities at birth (left side)	Improved muscle tone for balance and incontinence issues	Physical therapy (outside provider) one time monthly Home exercises three times weekly	Parents and physical therapist

Next Meeting Date: ___October 11___

Figure 5.10 Anna's pro-solve Tier 1 and 2 targeting process.

Student: ___Anna___   **Meeting Date:** ___October 11___

Participants: Ms. Meganski (special education teacher), Ms. Bailey (speech pathologist), Ms. Nicholson (special education aide), Mr. Markus (Avenues teacher/advisor), Ms. Lucas (high school counselor), Ms. Gengler (special education teacher)

Led by Teacher Teams	Targeted Outcomes	Desired Outcomes	Interventions and Action Steps	Who	Data Point 1	Data Point 2	Data Point 3	Data Point 4	Data Point 5
	Essential standards	Make correct change with 100% accuracy	Daily use of a purchase scenario question in math class Emphasis on this skill in speech sessions 3 times weekly	Ms. Meganski (self-contained math teacher) Ms. Bailey (speech pathologist)	Weekly tally sheet for math (1/5 correct) Weekly tally sheet for speech (1/3 correct)	Weekly tally sheet for math (0/5) Weekly tally sheet for speech (1/3)	Weekly tally sheet for math (0/5) Weekly tally sheet for speech (1/3)	Weekly tally sheet for math (1/5) Weekly tally sheet for speech (0/3)	Weekly tally sheet for math (2/5) Weekly tally sheet for speech (2/3)
	Immediate prerequisite skills	Be able to add and subtract numbers up to 100 without the use of manipulatives with 100% accuracy	Daily guided practice (20 minutes with aide) Daily self-directed math practice using mental math software	Ms. Nicholson (aide)	Weekly addition quiz (6/10) Weekly subtraction quiz (3/10)	Weekly addition quiz (6/10) Weekly subtraction quiz (5/10)	Weekly addition quiz (10/10) Weekly subtraction quiz (7/10) Begin work adding decimals	Weekly addition quiz (8/10) Weekly subtraction quiz (10/10)	Weekly addition quiz (9/10) Weekly subtraction quiz (10/10) Begin work subtracting decimals
	English language								

	Targeted Outcomes	Desired Outcomes	Interventions and Action Steps	Who	Data Point 1	Data Point 2	Data Point 3	Data Point 4	Data Point 5
Led by Schoolwide Teams	Academic behaviors	Assessment independence so Anna is not reliant on certain people for accurate assessment data (measured by Anna self-reporting on a 10-point scale)	Proctor coaching from trusted adult mentors	Ms. Nicholson and Ms. Meganski (strongest relationships)	Ms. Meganski and Ms. Nicholson proctor tests/quizzes but coach Anna (Anna reports 10/10)	Regular teacher proctors but Nicholson present (10/10)	Regular teacher proctors but Nicholson present (10/10)	Regular teacher proctors (10/10)	Anna agrees to give full effort if teachers stop "badgering her about this" Intervention ended
	Social behaviors	Initiates peer or community interactions for personal and life-skills purposes	Creation and mastery of three connection strategies / Creation and rehearsal of an emergency plan for incontinence issues	Ms. Lucas (counselor) creates and rehearses plan with Anna privately / Mr. Markus (advisory teacher) and Ms. Gengler (special education teacher) will monitor progress of connections. Anna will attempt a peer connection daily.	Advisory weekly checklist (2/2) / Ms. Gengler weekly checklist (2/5) / Incontinence plan rehearsal / In Ms. Gengler's class (1/1)	Advisory weekly checklist (2/2) / Ms. Gengler weekly checklist (3/5) / Incontinence plan rehearsal / In Ms. Gengler's class (1/1)	Advisory weekly checklist (2/2) / Ms. Gengler weekly checklist (3/5) / Incontinence plan rehearsal / In Mr. Markus's advisory (1/1)	Advisory weekly checklist (2/2) / Ms. Gengler weekly checklist (5/5) / Incontinence plan rehearsal / In Mr. Markus's advisory (1/1)	Advisory weekly checklist (2/2) / Ms. Gengler weekly checklist (5/5) / Incontinence plan rehearsal / In community (0/1, needs practice)
	Health and home	Improved muscle tone for balance and incontinence issues. No falls and no incontinence accidents 100% of the time.	Physical therapy (outside provider) one time monthly / Home exercises three times weekly	Parents and physical therapist	Workouts completed (3/3) / Falls (0) or accidents (0)	Workouts completed (1/3) / Falls (0) or accidents (0)	Workouts completed (0/3) / Falls (0) or accidents (0)	Workouts completed (1/3) / Falls (0) or accidents (1)	Workouts completed (3/3) / Falls (0) or accidents (0)

Next Meeting Date: October 25

Figure 5.11: Anna's pro-solve Tier 1 and 2 monitoring plan.

CHAPTER 6

Uniting Core Instruction and Intensive Remediation

I f a school provides students access to essential grade-level curriculum and effective initial teaching during Tier 1 core instruction, and targeted supplemental academic and behavioral help in meeting these standards at Tier 2, then most students should be succeeding. But there will inevitably be a number of students who are still struggling because they lack the critical foundational skills needed to learn at all. These universal skills of learning include:

- **Reading**—The ability to decode and comprehend text is a foundational skill to virtually all learning, as there is hardly a grade level, course, or subject that does not require a student to learn information through written text. Subsequently, a student significantly below grade level in reading ability is at risk throughout the entire school day.

- **Writing**—Like reading, most grade levels, subjects, and courses require a student to demonstrate understanding and apply thinking in a written format. For this reason, a student's ability to express his or her thoughts through writing is a universal skill of learning. When students are significantly below grade level in this skill, it will negatively affect their academic achievement across the curriculum.

- **Number sense**—Number sense is shown through a student's ability to demonstrate a feel for numbers, sequencing, mathematical functions, and mastery of grade-level-appropriate foundational math skills. Number sense is a learning leverage skill that stretches across the curriculum. For example, try to teach a student without number sense how to use the periodic table, read a timeline in history, double a recipe in culinary arts, or determine heart rate in physical education—it would be almost impossible for the student to learn these specific curricular standards without number sense.

- **English language**—As a vast majority of classes in the U.S. public school system are taught in English, students without at least basic conversational skills find learning any content an impossibility. Students without foundational skills in English will require intensive help.

- **Basic academic and social behaviors**—As mentioned in the previous section on Tier 2, academic and social behaviors are the self-monitoring and social skills and dispositions necessary for a student to succeed at school. Students in need of Tier 3 support in those areas are so lacking in these behaviors that they find it consistently difficult to demonstrate them in almost every school setting.

- **Health and home**—At Tier 3, students who need intensive interventions are facing extreme health issues or a family crisis. Examples could include a student who is severely diabetic and without proper monitoring, may not only miss potential class time but face life-threatening consequences. Or a student may have a parent who is terminally ill. Such severe adversity may require intensive health or counseling services.

These universal skills represent much more than a student needing help in a specific learning standard, but instead they represent a series of skills that enable a student to comprehend instruction, access information, demonstrate understanding, and behaviorally function in a school setting. If a student is significantly behind in just one of these universal skills, he or she will struggle in virtually every grade level, course, and subject, and usually a school's most at-risk youth are behind in more than one.

Elementary schools do not assume that students entering kindergarten possess basic literacy, numeracy, and self-monitoring skills, so these universal skills comprise most of the grade-level essential standards in the primary grades. Due to this schoolwide focus in the early years of school, most students enter upper grades with at least an adequate level of mastery in these foundational skills.

Beyond the primary grades, schools generally assume that students entering upper elementary, middle, and high school already possess these universal skills, and so does the state grade-level curriculum. For students who have not mastered these skills, they will need intensive instruction to catch up, but these foundational skills are no longer part of grade-level core instruction. If these students are pulled from essential grade-level curriculum to receive this remedial support, they will never close their achievement gaps. For every remedial skill they make up, they will likely miss new, critical grade-level standards; this is equivalent to "one step forward, one step back."

If a school is dedicated to having its most at-risk students learn at high levels, it must create a system of tiered support in which students have access to grade-level essential standards, supplemental support in meeting these standards, and intensive interventions in foundational skills—"the core and more and more." The key consideration is that *more* represents not only more intensive instruction but also access to additional targeted, tiered learning outcomes. The RTI at Work pyramid (figure 6.1, page 110) captures this concept with the learning outcomes band along the right-hand side of the pyramid.

Determining the individual needs of a school's most at-risk youth, creating a master schedule that provides multiple tiers of support, and allocating the resources necessary to achieve these outcomes will require schoolwide efforts. For this reason, we recommend two essential schoolwide teams take lead responsibility for Tier 3 interventions.

Two Critical Teams

While teacher teams focus on specific grade and subject learning outcomes, we recommend that two *schoolwide collaborative teams*—a site leadership team and an intervention team—be responsible for coordinating intensive interventions across the school. The *school leadership team* serves as the guiding coalition for the building. Comprised of representatives from each collaborative teacher team, administration, and classified and support staff, this team's primary responsibility is to unite and coordinate the school's collective efforts across grade levels, departments, and subjects. To achieve this goal, the school leadership team should specifically:

- Build consensus for the school's mission of collective responsibility

- Create a master schedule that provides sufficient time for team collaboration, core instruction, supplemental interventions, and intensive interventions

- Coordinate schoolwide human resources to best support core instruction and interventions, including the site counselor, psychologist, speech and language pathologist, special education teacher, librarian, health services, subject specialists, instructional aides, and other classified staff

- Allocate the school's fiscal resources to best support core instruction and interventions, including school categorical funding

- Assist with articulating essential learning outcomes across grade levels and subjects

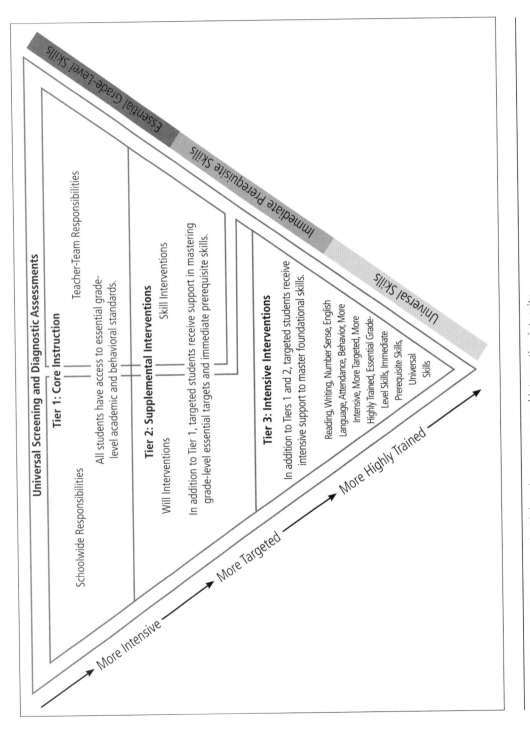

Figure 6.1: The RTI at Work pyramid with learning outcomes and intervention intensity.

Visit **go.solution-tree.com/rtiatwork** *for a reproducible version of this figure.*

- Lead the school's universal screening efforts to identify students in need of Tier 3 intensive interventions before they fail

- Lead the school's efforts at Tier 1 for schoolwide behavioral expectations, including attendance policies and awards and recognitions (the team may create a separate behavior team to oversee these behavioral policies)

- Ensure that all students have access to grade-level core instruction

- Ensure that sufficient, effective resources are available to provide Tier 2 interventions for students in need of supplemental support in motivation, attendance, and behavior

- Ensure that sufficient, effective resources are available to provide Tier 3 interventions for students in need of intensive support in the universal skills of reading, writing, number sense, English language, motivation, attendance, and behavior

- Continually monitor schoolwide evidence of student learning

Without question, the leadership team has critically important responsibilities that greatly affect the entire school. This is why we stress that it is this team's job to lead—not to dictate. It should unite the school's staff toward their mission of collective responsibility and coordinate the school's limited resources to best achieve this goal.

While this leadership team is responsible for the larger schoolwide structures that support student learning, the *school intervention team*'s primary responsibility is to coordinate the school's efforts to meet the needs of individual students requiring intensive support. The primary purpose of an intervention team is not to be the gatekeeper to special education testing—it is to focus intensively on the individual needs of a school's most at-risk students. Consequently, the primary responsibilities of the site intervention team are to:

- Determine the specific learning needs of each student in need of intensive support

- Diagnose the causes of the student's struggles in Tier 1 and Tier 2

- Determine the most appropriate interventions to address the student's needs

- Frequently monitor the student's progress to see if interventions are achieving the desired outcomes

- Revise the student's interventions when he or she is not achieving the desired outcomes

- Determine when special education identification is appropriate

Because students in need of intensive support usually have multiple needs, it is important that the intervention team is comprised of site experts in the specific areas that cause students to struggle in school. When determining who should serve on this team, membership should include the site or district professionals who have the greatest expertise in each of the universal skills. The activity in figure 6.2 for building a site intervention team is designed to provide clarity on the essential membership roles that should be included to create an effective intervention team, as well as recommendations regarding common site personnel who are frequently best trained to meet each role.

As is the case with Tier 2, a school must have a frequent, systematic process to identify students who potentially need intensive interventions. Creating a timely response will necessitate that the intervention team create a frequent meeting schedule, especially considering that some of the members on the intervention team might not be on a school's campus every day, such as a school psychologist or speech and language pathologist.

While the leadership and intervention teams are complementary, they serve two markedly different purposes. The school leadership team is taking the larger "macro view" of not only site interventions, but your entire school program. They are not using their meeting time to discuss the individual needs of each at-risk student, but instead are focusing on coordinating the schoolwide master schedule, team efforts, and support staff. The purpose of the intervention team is to focus on the individual needs of specific students—the "micro view" of interventions.

There may be times in which the intervention team determines the needs of a particular student, but the school currently does not have the resources allotted to address the need, so the leadership team will need to discuss and reallocate resources. This is why we recommend that the principal be on both teams. The principal has the greatest impact on determining resources, and so he or she can facilitate and coordinate between the two teams.

Identifying Students for Intensive Interventions

Considering that students in need of Tier 3 supports are already alarmingly behind in school, delays in providing intensive interventions will only make a bad situation even worse. Universal screening practices can be used to proactively identify these students. The primary purpose of universal screening is to identify students in need of intensive support. This outcome can be achieved either by a short, quick assessment tied to a universal skill (reading, writing, math sense, or English learning), or if the student is already at your school or district, the current staff most likely can identify these students. Universal screening does not need to involve a test, and you don't need to do a universal screening three times a year. While there may be skills, scenarios, and grade levels for which formal assessments and increased screening may be

Team Members: _____

Essential Role	Recommended	Staff Members Best Trained to Meet This Need
Administration	Principal	
Reading	Reading specialist	
Writing	ELA specialist	
Math	Math specialist	
English language	EL specialist	
Language	Speech and language pathologist	
Teaching differentiation	Special education teacher	
Behavior	Psychologist	
Social, family	Counselor	
Instructional resources	Librarian	
Community resources	Community resource officer Social worker Counselor	

When will this team meet? (Determine a weekly meeting time and location.)

Time: _____   Location: _____

Team norms: _____

_____

_____

Figure 6.2: Tool for creating a site intervention team.

*Visit **go.solution-tree.com/rtiatwork** for a reproducible version of this figure.*

appropriate, we must remember why we do universal screening: to identify students at extreme risk of failing before we ever begin core instruction. There is no excuse for a school to start a new school year without plans in place for Tier 3 supports that will begin within the first days of school. We can put processes in place to identify students with significant deficits in foundational skills, students who will require Tier 3 supports, before the end of each school year, in preparation for the next year. We can plan for schedules, personnel, and resources to provide these supports. We can avoid the surprise when students fail, again, due to significant deficits. We can predict the identity of students who are at risk and the supports they will need. We can prevent the cycle of reactionary, panicked interventions started in November, when we could have started proactive supports in September.

The global nature of the required skills suggests that the schoolwide leadership team should take the lead on this process. And, after all, the schoolwide leadership team takes the lead on overseeing Tier 3 interventions, the interventions that will be required for students who are screened and found to have significant deficits in foundational skills. In *Simplifying Response to Intervention* (Buffum et al., 2012), we provide a Universal Screening Planning Guide (figure 6.3) for a process schools can use to identify students requiring intensive supports.

Here is the key point regarding universal screening—it is a quick identification process used to identify students, but it is not enough information to place these students into the proper intervention. Students struggling in reading are not all struggling for the same reason—so there is no "one size fits all" reading intervention for these students. Once the students are identified, the school intervention team will utilize the pro-solve process to determine the specific needs for each student.

The Universal Screening Planning Guide activity is designed to assist a leadership team plan for universal screening by creating a process to identify students in need of intensive support *before* they fail. Because the purpose is to provide preventive support, it is best if this activity is completed prior to the start of the school year.

For each universal skill, answer questions for each column.

1. **At-Risk Criteria:** At each grade level, what criteria will be used to determine whether a child is in need of intensive support? For example, in reading, an elementary school may determine that any student entering first grade without the ability to properly recognize all twenty-six letters (uppercase and lowercase) is extremely at risk in reading and will be considered for immediate, intensive support. At a high school, any student whose reading ability is two or more years below grade level (grade-level equivalent) could be considered for immediate, intensive support.

Universal Skill	At-Risk Criteria What criteria will be used to determine whether a child is in need of intensive support?	Screening Process What screening assessment and/or process will be used to identify students in need of intensive support?	When When will the screening process take place?	Who Who will administer the screening?	Intensive Support Available What intensive intervention(s) will be used to accelerate student learning and support the identified student(s)?
Reading					
Writing					
Number sense					
English language					
Attendance					
Behavior					

Figure 6.3: Universal screening planning guide.

*Visit **go.solution-tree.com/rtiatwork** for a reproducible version of this figure.*

2. **Screening Process:** What screening assessment and/or process will be used to identify students in need of intensive support? The leadership team should identify the most effective, efficient, and timely process to gather the at-risk criteria data on each student.

3. **When:** When will the screening process take place? Obviously, if the purpose of universal screening is to provide preventive support, then this data should be collected either prior to the start of the school year or as early in the school year as possible. Finally, as new students will enroll in the school throughout the year, it is important to consider how these students can be screened during the enrollment process.

4. **Who:** Who will administer the screening? As the leadership team has representation from every teacher team, as well as responsibility for coordinating school support staff, this team is best positioned to organize the resources necessary.

5. **Intensive Support Available:** What intensive intervention(s) will be used to accelerate student learning and support the identified student(s)? There is no point in universal screening if there is no plan to provide these students extra support in their area(s) of need.

One final consideration: for a school new to universal screening, it may be overwhelming to begin universal screening in all six universal skills, at all grade levels, immediately. In this case, we recommend that the leadership team identify the universal skill (reading, writing, number sense, English language, attendance, behavior) that is currently the greatest area of need in their school. Start by focusing on this one. As the school builds skill and competence in this area, others can be added.

Applying the Pro-Solve Process to Tier 3

The intervention team will use the pro-solve process to guide their efforts. While the curricular outcomes are different for supplemental and intensive interventions, the pro-solve targeting process to diagnose a specific student's unique needs is the same.

The students most at risk in a school are not lacking in only one universal skill; they usually have multiple areas of need, often in both skill and will. Led by the school intervention team, the same pro-solve process is used at Tier 3 to diagnose a targeted student's needs, but the learning outcomes will be different from those listed in the

Tier 2 pro-solve protocol. Instead, the learning outcomes are the Tier 3 universal skills, as shown in figure 6.4 (page 118) and figure 6.5 (page 119).

Tier 3 supports are designed to provide intensive help to students with significant deficits in foundational or universal skills. We define universal academic skills as reading, number sense, writing, and English language acquisition. When the screening of a student reveals significant difficulties, we diagnose to determine the causes of those difficulties. For example:

- A grade 4 student cannot decode monosyllabic words, which significantly impacts fluency and comprehension of text in any content area.

- A grade 7 student lacks conceptual and procedural knowledge of place value and the conservation of numbers, which impacts success with any topic in mathematics, as well as knowledge of timelines in social studies, the periodic table in science, and heart rate in physical education.

- A grade 9 student cannot write an intelligible sentence, one with correct subject-verb agreement, spelling, capitalization, and punctuation, which impacts success with demonstrating mastery in any content area.

- A grade 6 student has been attending U.S. schools since kindergarten, learning English as a second language. His peers have been designated as English proficient or as advanced English learners, but this grade 6 student is still assessed in the early intermediate range. A significant deficit in the rate of English language acquisition will impact success with both receptive and expressive language in every content area.

When students are screened and diagnosed to possess significant deficits with foundational skills, they must receive intensive Tier 3 supports. When Tier 1 and supplemental Tier 2 supports are not resulting in student mastery of essentials, we must consider that deficits in foundational skills may be the cause, necessitating intensive Tier 3 supports. Tier 3 supports are targeted on foundational skills, and there are progress-monitoring assessments specially designed for measuring progress on these skills. These are known as curriculum-based measurements, or CBMs. We recommend that schoolwide teams efficiently organize Tier 3 progress-monitoring data. A sample Tier 3 progress-monitoring form for organizing literacy data appears in figure 6.6 (page 120).

Student: _____   **Meeting Date:** _____

Participants: _____

Targeted Outcomes	1. Concern	2. Cause	3. Desired Outcomes	4. Intervention Steps	5. Who Takes Responsibility
Led by Intervention Team Foundational reading skills					
Foundational number sense					
Foundational writing					
Foundational language					
Academic behaviors					
Social behaviors					
Health and home					

Next Meeting Date: _____

Figure 6.4: RTI at Work pro-solve intervention targeting process—Tier 3.

*Visit **go.solution-tree.com/rtiatwork** for a reproducible version of this figure.*

Student: _____   **Meeting Date:** _____

Participants: _____

Targeted Outcomes	Desired Outcomes	Interventions and Action Steps	Who	Data Point 1	Data Point 2	Data Point 3	Data Point 4	Data Point 5
Led by Intervention Team	Foundational reading skills							
	Foundational number sense							
	Foundational writing							
	Foundational language							
	Academic behaviors							
	Social behaviors							
	Health and home							

Next Meeting Date: _____

Figure 6.5: RTI at Work pro-solve intervention monitoring plan—Tier 3.

*Visit **go.solution-tree.com/rtiatwork** for a reproducible version of this figure.*

Foundational Skill	Description	Progress-monitoring							
		Mastery	Mastery	Mastery	Mastery	Mastery	Mastery	Mastery	Mastery
		Reading							
Phonological awareness									
Monosyllabic phonics									
Multisyllabic phonics									
Fluency									
Explicit comprehension									
Implicit comprehension									
		Writing							
Legibility									
Spacing									
Punctuation									
Subject-verb agreement									
Organization									
Spelling									
Coherent idea									

Figure 6.6: Progress-monitoring chart.

Visit **go.solution-tree.com/rtiatwork** *for a reproducible version of this figure.*

Unlike other assessments, CBMs are designed to:

- Be sensitive to small improvements

- Allow for multiple administrations through the use of alternate versions

- Be brief, making them efficient to administer

- Assess specific skills that represent a broader domain, such as a pseudoword fluency assessment for the domain of phonics

- Allow for trend lines to be compared to norm-referenced aim lines, which allows student performance to be compared to the student's past performance and a target

To accurately determine the extent to which a student is responding to Tier 3 interventions, select CBMs that match the student's current level of need and support, which may not be the student's current grade level. A selected CBM should also best match the skill area in which the student is currently receiving support.

While CBMs are specially designed assessments, schools need not spend a great deal of money on them; they can often be found for free or at little cost. While they are specially designed, they should not be misapplied. They are simply intended to monitor response to intensive, targeted supports—student response to Tier 3 intervention. Teams enter the evolving responses of students to interventions in the right-hand columns marked "mastery."

When students require intensive behavior supports to address deficits in foundational behavioral skills—when there is evidence that changes and adaptations to adult behaviors are not sufficient to help students be successful—then more diagnostic information is necessary to determine more targeted interventions. If students have not responded to the types of schoolwide behavior supports described in chapter 4 and the types of supplemental Tier 2 behavior interventions defined in chapter 5, then the school must take bold and compassionate action to help the student to succeed. This will necessitate a more formal data-gathering process.

In chapter 5 of this book and in two previous books, *Pyramid of Behavior Interventions* (Hierck et al., 2011) and *Simplifying Response to Intervention* (Buffum et al., 2012), we described a simplified functional behavioral analysis, or FBA. This brief but informative exercise provides critical information regarding the causes and purposes of student misbehaviors when completed collaboratively by staff. To determine the most appropriate and targeted Tier 3 supports, a formal FBA or similarly detailed and diagnostic assessment should be completed. These assessments will require weeks of observations, data gathering, and discussions and should be led by qualified staff members, typically school psychologists. The benefits of making a commitment to a formal FBA can be enormous; they will inform the collaborative design of a targeted behavior intervention plan (BIP) that a student's continuing difficulties have made necessary.

A BIP is designed to provide the greatest degree of specificity regarding expectations, consequences, and procedures related to a student's behavioral needs. It typically includes the following elements.

- The desired target behavior, clearly identified and described

- The opposite of each appropriate behavior, the misbehaviors that have not yet been successfully modified, clearly identified, and described

- Strategies and skills required to display the desired behaviors, which are taught and consistently modeled by all adults

- Ongoing, targeted, and intensive supports that address the diagnosed needs and functions of the misbehaviors

- Academic deficits that emerge through diagnoses of needs, which are remediated with appropriate interventions

- Positive reinforcement when students display desired behaviors, and cumulative reinforcement when students reach predefined thresholds associated with displaying the desired behaviors

- Clear and appropriate consequences for misbehavior that are consistently enforced in a timely manner

- Corrective action to be initiated as a consequence, including:
    - Reteaching
    - Reflection
    - Knowledge of impact
    - Restitution

As noted earlier in this book, CBMs are progress-monitoring assessments specially designed for measuring the progress of students in foundational skills. As we noted earlier, the choice of what type of CBM will be made clearer when teams have diagnosed the causes of student difficulty and provided targeted interventions that address these causes. CBMs should be selected that match the student's current level of need and support and the skill area in which the student is currently receiving support. These specially designed, sensitive, brief probes that simply measure student progress in response to receiving intensive, targeted supports—student response to Tier 3 intervention—can often be found for free or at little cost.

Check-in/check-out (CI/CO) can be used to monitor student progress with intensive behavior supports. Both a monitoring and a mentoring tool, CI/CO is a simple, powerful process that produces timely data that can be used to measure the effectiveness of the strategy and student progress.

Our goal is high levels of learning for all students, whatever it takes. When students are not initially responding to Tier 3 interventions, provided concurrently with differentiated Tier 1 and Tier 2 supports, we must collaboratively determine the reasons and revise the intensity of supports. Increasing the intensity of interventions may require that we adjust the:

- Frequency and duration of interventions

- Specific areas that interventions are targeting

- Student-to-teacher ratio in which interventions are provided

- Quality and quantity of professional development for staff to meet diagnosed needs

Increasingly, we believe that the most critical factor in successfully meeting student needs is how precisely and successfully we are targeting a student's needs. The more targeted the intervention, the better the intervention. Determining the causes of student difficulties will allow us to determine the most appropriately targeted support. Let's explore how this targeted, "core and more and more" approach is translated into specific interventions for Armando, Katie, Holly, Franklin, and Anna.

Armando and Robinson Elementary

The collaborative efforts of Armando's teacher team have partially met his academic needs. With Tier 1 and Tier 2 supports, his comprehension of text, mathematics abilities, and social behaviors are improving. While he is not falling further behind in the area of phonics, the gap is not closing. Screening at the end of kindergarten and at the beginning of first grade identified Armando with significant deficits in the foundational skill of phonics. Robinson Elementary's schoolwide team began the process of diagnosing the causes of these difficulties, while also supporting the teacher team in its efforts to provide the necessary supports for Armando at Tiers 1 and 2. Armando's teacher team has reported that he has yet to respond to Tier 1 and 2 levels of support; the schoolwide team believes it has diagnosed possible causes for these difficulties.

Use of the CORE Phonics Survey confirmed that Armando had difficulty decoding even CVC (consonant-vowel-consonant) words. While he consistently knows letter names, he has more difficulty with sounds. The schoolwide team's administration of the CORE Phonological Segmentation Test revealed that he had difficulty processing sounds orally. His skills identifying the initial, medial, and ending sounds of words were well below where the team would expect a first grader to perform. These difficulties seemed likely to contribute to difficulties decoding the written word. These diagnoses matched teacher observations. Armando has trouble paying attention to and remembering information presented orally. He experiences confusion when asked to follow multistep directions. Given these observations, the team developed a plan to provide Armando with Tier 3 interventions to supplement the Tier 1 and 2 supports that he will continue to receive.

Ms. Flood, the school's special education teacher, already provides supports to students in kindergarten through second grade with difficulties in early reading. The supports that she provides meet the characteristics that Armando presents. Ms. Flood can provide supports to Armando either during the thirty minutes right before lunch or during the thirty minutes right after lunch. Ms. Hollings provides instruction in social studies right before lunch, and Armando attends electives right after lunch. Ms. Flood meets with intervention groups during both time periods. Ms. Flood will vary when she provides supports to Armando from week to week, so that he does not miss the opportunity to attend either social studies or specials for an extended period. The teams agree, however, that the priority for Armando at this stage is to receive intensive supports in reading. In the absence of targeted, alternative phonics supports, Armando's difficulties will become cumulatively more significant.

Ms. Flood's groups consist of students with IEPs and those like Armando who have not been determined eligible for special education services. She differentiates and targets supports based on student needs. In general, she approaches early reading from a nontraditional perspective. She uses alternatives to synthetic phonics, for example, to support students in their decoding of words.

Ms. Flood also employs multimodal approaches, using feedback to allow students to understand the shapes and movements of their mouths when producing sounds. She ensures that the study of reading involves multisensory opportunities—that connections are made through simultaneous auditory, visual, and kinesthetic reinforcements. Finally, Armando engages with a computer-based intervention that exercises his memory and attention while improving his abilities at processing and sequencing. The team teachers remind one another constantly that, while critically important to Armando's present and future reading, phonics is only a means to the end. The ultimate goal of all reading instruction is comprehension, and all teachers who work with Armando continually reinforce the importance of making meaning of words and text.

To ensure the success of Tier 3 interventions, Ms. Hollings began monitoring Armando's progress by measuring his rate, accuracy, and prosody when reading pre-primer texts. The team decided that using a traditional nonsense-word fluency CBM to monitor RTI would not make sense in this case. Armando's rate of progress in response to Tier 1, Tier 2, and Ms. Flood's Tier 3 supports has resulted in rapid gains in reading, as measured by Ms. Hollings's weekly assessments. Armando met pre-primer norms within five weeks of first receiving Tier 3 supports. He was graduated to primer text and continues to make progress. The goal is to have him accurately and expressively reading first-grade text at an appropriate rate by the middle of second grade. He's well on his way. Figure 6.7 (page 126) and figure 6.8 (page 127) are examples of Armando's completed pro-solve process and subsequent monitoring plan data for Tier 3.

Katie and Wilson Elementary

Katie's social-emotional needs are increasingly impacting her academic performance and mental health. Working with Katie's mother, the principal and the school intervention team set a plan in action to provide wraparound supports for Katie, based on the school psychologist's and Mrs. Martin's diagnoses of needs.

The school principal and Mrs. Martin have worked with district personnel to connect Katie's mom with community-based counseling supports. There are free counseling supports for which Katie and her family are eligible, given her father's military deployment. Katie and the rest of her family have started attending weekly supports with a family resource center near Wilson Elementary. Katie's mom has given permission for the outside counselor to collaborate with the school psychologist and Mrs. Martin so that in-school and out-of-school supports can be coordinated.

Next, while Katie is adequately responding to Tier 2 academic supports, the team teachers have agreed that proactive Tier 3 supports in fluency and comprehension would be wise to initiate. They hope that these more intensive supports will serve two important functions: Katie's comprehension is a consistent area of concern, and more targeted supports in a smaller group, provided in addition to Tier 1 and 2 comprehension instruction, should prevent her from dipping below adequate levels of mastery, which would likely exacerbate her motivational and emotional deficits. The second purpose of this Tier 3 support is to give Katie more opportunities for positive feedback and attention in a small-group setting. In other words, her teachers hope that this reading intervention will meet both Katie's comprehension needs and her emotional needs.

Student: Armando

Meeting Date: November 12

Participants: Ms. Hollings (first grade), Mr. Stahl (kindergarten), Ms. Walker (second grade), Mrs. Curso (counselor), Ms. Gephardt (principal), Ms. Flood (special education teacher)

	Targeted Outcomes	**1. Concern**	**2. Cause**	**3. Desired Outcomes**	**4. Intervention Steps**	**5. Who Takes Responsibility**
Led by Intervention Team	Foundational reading skills	Phonological awareness and early phonics	Suspect auditory processing difficulties	Ability to hear and process sounds to decode text Ability to decode first-grade text accurately, with the appropriate rate, and the appropriate expression	Alternative phonics; multimodal, multisensory approaches; and computer-based intervention (memory, attention, processing, and sequencing)	Ms. Flood
	Foundational number sense					
	Foundational writing					
	Foundational language					
	Academic behaviors					
	Social behaviors					
	Health and home					

Next Meeting Date: November 26

Figure 6.7: Armando's pro-solve Tier 3 targeting process.

Student: Armando   **Meeting Date:** November 26

Participants: Ms. Hollings (first grade), Mr. Stahl (kindergarten), Ms. Walker (second grade), Mrs. Curso (counselor), Ms. Gephardt (principal), Ms. Flood (special education teacher)

	Targeted Outcomes	Desired Outcomes	Interventions and Action Steps	Who	Data Point 1	Data Point 2	Data Point 3	Data Point 4	Data Point 5
Led by Intervention Team	Foundational reading skills	Ability to hear and process sounds to decode text Ability to decode first-grade text accurately, with the appropriate rate, and the appropriate expression	Alternative phonics; multimodal, multisensory approaches; and computer-based intervention (memory, attention, processing, and sequencing)	Ms. Flood	Preprimer text ORF (13 wcpm)	Preprimer text ORF (23 wcpm)	Primer text ORF (14 wcpm)		
	Foundational number sense								
	Foundational writing								
	Foundational language								
	Academic behaviors								
	Social behaviors								
	Health and home								

Next Meeting Date: December 13

Source: Created by Mike Mattos.

Figure 6.8: Armando's pro-solve Tier 3 monitoring plan.

The school has also recommitted to leveraging the staff's collective responsibility on behalf of Katie. In addition to Mr. Beyer, Ms. Hendricks, and the other fourth-grade teachers, the third-grade teachers with whom Katie worked last year have devised a plan to regularly check in with Katie in a natural, unobtrusive way. The goal is to ensure that Katie knows that there are multiple adults on campus who care for her.

Finally, Mrs. Martin is training the school's social worker, Ms. Mariner, in leading two sessions with Katie each week. The first session will be a small group with Katie and her peers with a focus on building healthy interpersonal relationships. The second, one-on-one session will allow Katie and Ms. Mariner to work on the trauma that Katie is experiencing, using a curriculum called Cognitive Behavioral Intervention for Trauma in Schools (RAND Corporation, 2013), for which both Mrs. Martin and Ms. Mariner have received training.

The school, in partnership with Katie's mom and district and community organizations, is providing a suite of tiered supports for Katie. While concerns still exist, the team believes that Katie's initial response to these interventions suggests that emotional and academic successes are inevitable. Figure 6.9 and figure 6.10 (page 130) are examples of Katie's completed pro-solve process and subsequent monitoring plan data for Tier 3.

Holly and Roosevelt Elementary

Roosevelt Elementary School's commitment to collective responsibility extends to all students, including students with special education needs and those with more severe disabilities. The school motto is "We provide supports to students based on need, not label; educators support students based on staff expertise, not title." Holly receives Tier 3 supports in reading and behavior with grade-alike peers at Roosevelt.

Students with significant deficits in comprehension receive targeted supports using aresearch-based intervention. Students receive supports based on their current levels of readiness, not necessarily their grade level. Holly participates in a group with students from fourth, fifth, and sixth grade, all of whom have reading levels in the second- to third-grade range. Holly is supported within these sessions by an instructional assistant, Mr. Ramirez, who is proficient in American Sign Language. She can follow the guided reading process that the interventionist (who is a school reading specialist) utilizes. She participates in the focused comprehension investigations, contributing to discussions by signing to the assistant, who shares with the group. While she was hesitant to participate at first, she now regularly contributes.

Student: Katie   **Meeting Date:** November 12

Participants: Mr. Beyer (fourth grade), Ms. Hendricks (fourth grade), Mrs. Crist (fourth grade), Mrs. McKeown (fourth grade), Ms. Wilson (fourth grade), Mrs. Cook (fourth grade), Mrs. Martin (district counselor), Ms. Mariner (social worker), Mr. Fraunheim (principal)

	Targeted Outcomes	1. Concern	2. Cause	3. Desired Outcomes	4. Intervention Steps	5. Who Takes Responsibility
Led by Intervention Team	Foundational reading skills					
	Foundational number sense					
	Foundational writing					
	Foundational language					
	Academic behaviors	Withdrawn and seemingly unmotivated	Father deployed frequently	Self-regulated and self-motivated learner	Mentoring sessions with Ms. Hendricks	Ms. Hendricks
	Social behaviors					
	Health and home	Social-emotional responses to dad's deployment	Father deployed frequently	Positive outlook on life	Support of district counselor	Mrs. Martin

Next Meeting Date: November 26

Figure 6.9: Katie's pro-solve Tier 3 targeting process.

Student: Katie

Meeting Date: November 26

Participants: Mr. Beyer (fourth grade), Ms. Hendricks (fourth grade), Mrs. Crist (fourth grade), Mrs. McKeown (fourth grade), Ms. Wilson (fourth grade), Mrs. Cook (fourth grade), Mrs. Martin (district counselor), Ms. Mariner (social worker), Mr. Fraunheim (principal)

	Targeted Outcomes	Desired Outcomes	Interventions and Action Steps	Who	Data Point 1	Data Point 2	Data Point 3	Data Point 4	Data Point 5
Led by Intervention Team	Foundational reading skills				Preprimer text ORF (13 wcpm)	Preprimer text ORF (23 wcpm)	Primer text ORF (14 wcpm)		
	Foundational number sense								
	Foundational writing								
	Foundational language								
	Academic behaviors	Self-regulated and self-motivated learner	Mentoring sessions with Ms. Hendricks	Ms. Hendricks					
	Social behaviors								
	Health and home	Positive outlook on life	Support of district counselor	Mrs. Martin	Surveys completed by teachers, parent, and student (21-point scale, 15-point average, high risk)	Surveys completed by teachers, parent, and student (21-point scale, 12-point average, high risk)	Surveys completed by teachers, parent, and student (21-point scale, 8-point average, medium risk)		

Next Meeting Date: December 13

Figure 6.10: Katie's pro-solve Tier 3 monitoring plan.

In addition, Holly attends a weekly social-skills group with other fifth- and sixth-grade students. The school's counselor leads these groups, and Holly's classmates are empathetic role models. Holly's socialization skills are improving, and her interactions with nondisabled peers have led to a decrease in stemming-type behaviors. Mr. Ramirez accompanies Holly to this weekly group.

As a result of the suite of Tier 1, 2, and 3 supports that Holly receives from a wide cross section of Roosevelt staff, she is making steady progress toward her goals. In addition, the team, along with Holly and her mom and dad, feels confident and excited about her transition to junior high. Figure 6.11 (page 132) and figure 6.12 (page 133) are examples of Holly's completed pro-solve process and subsequent monitoring plan data for Tier 3.

Franklin and Middletown Middle School

Franklin's Tier 3 challenges can be summed up in one word: *inattentiveness*. This has taken the form of constant disruption in class, calling out, daydreaming, and his being easily distracted. In his first class of the day, a squirrel in the tree outside so intrigued him that little else was accomplished during the day. Over time, he has used such events to engage his teachers in escalations that ultimately provided him with what he wanted: removal from classes that he routinely found nonstimulating.

The members of his collaborative teacher team want to leverage the success they feel they have achieved with their Tier 2 interventions regarding his academic behaviors, and believe the first step is to provide Franklin with a visible, tangible schedule of the lessons or activities of the day. They are attempting to match what they see as his learning style with their instructional pedagogy to improve his on-task behavior and keep the lessons moving at a brisk pace. They know Franklin becomes more distracted when time is spent on housekeeping items and during transitions. They are ensuring that instruction is structured through full lesson preparation and have removed all items in Franklin's immediate area that are not needed for tasks.

They also have noticed Franklin is more engaged when they capture his attention early. They are employing predictable structures, routines, and procedures and reinforcing auditory directions with pictures and other visual supports. They ensure they gain Franklin's attention before giving directions. So as not to single Franklin out, they employ classwide strategies that are effective for all students. They call students by name and establish eye contact before providing the directions. They use alerting cues to gain attention and wait until all students are attentive before giving directions.

Student: Holly

Meeting Date: November 12

Participants: Ms. Blackburn (special education teacher), Ms. O'Connor (general education teacher), Mrs. Banning (special education teacher), Ms. Breo (principal), Mr. Ramirez (instructional assistant)

	Targeted Outcomes	1. Concern	2. Cause	3. Desired Outcomes	4. Intervention Steps	5. Who Takes Responsibility
Led by Intervention Team	Foundational reading skills	Decoding	Nonverbal	Read an increasing number of words by sight	Edmark	Ms. Blackburn
	Foundational number sense	Correspondence, cardinality, counting, composition, and conservation	Nonverbal	Represent and manipulate numbers to 100	Every Day Counts	Ms. Blackburn
	Foundational writing					
	Foundational language					
	Academic behaviors	Significant difficulties with executive functioning	Communicative difficulties attributable to autism	Improved self-advocacy when navigating daily schedules	Visual and guided task-completion checklists	Mr. Ramirez / Ms. Blackburn
	Social behaviors	Outbursts when faced with new situations	Social anxieties attributable to autism	Self-monitoring and self-regulating of behaviors	Social-skills group	Counselor / Mr. Ramirez / Ms. Blackburn
	Health and home					

Next Meeting Date: November 26

Figure 6.11: Holly's pro-solve Tier 3 targeting process.

Student: Holly

Meeting Date: November 26

Participants: Ms. Blackburn (special education teacher), Ms. O'Connor (general education teacher), Mrs. Banning (special education teacher) Ms. Breo (principal), Mr. Ramirez (instructional assistant)

Led by Intervention Team	Targeted Outcomes	Desired Outcomes	Interventions and Action Steps	Who	Data Point 1	Data Point 2	Data Point 3	Data Point 4	Data Point 5
	Foundational reading skills	Read an increasing number of words by sight	Edmark	Ms. Blackburn	Dolch Sight Words (grade 2)—29 wcpm	Dolch Sight Words (grade 3)—35 wcpm	Dolch Sight Words (grade 3)—40 wcpm		
	Foundational number sense	Represent and manipulate numbers to 100	Every Day Counts	Ms. Blackburn	Number decomposition—11	Number decomposition—13	Number decomposition—16		
	Foundational writing								
	Foundational language								
	Academic behaviors	Improved self-advocacy when navigating daily schedules	Visual and guided task-completion checklists	Mr. Ramirez Ms. Blackburn	CI/CO goal of navigating daily routines (average of 10 daily points/week)	CI/CO goal of navigating daily routines (average of 13 daily points/week)	CI/CO goal of navigating daily routines (average of 15 daily points/week)		
	Social behaviors	Self-monitoring and self-regulating of behaviors	Social-skills group	Counselor Mr. Ramirez Ms. Blackburn	CI/CO goal self-monitoring (average of 10 daily points/week)	CI/CO goal self-monitoring (average of 11 daily points/week)	CI/CO goal self-monitoring (average of 10 daily points/week)		
	Health and home								

Next Meeting Date: December 13

Figure 6.12: Holly's pro-solve Tier 3 monitoring plan.

For Franklin specifically, they proactively and privately approach him and reiterate and restate directions, asking him to repeat directions.

As mentioned, the team provides Franklin the option to take attention breaks. The teachers have created a contract with Franklin to give him short breaks to engage in a preferred activity each time that he finishes a given amount of work. They suspect that these attention breaks refresh Franklin and make the learning task more reinforced. As his attentive behavior improves, they will modify the contract.

The team has also expressed some concerns that the ongoing misbehavior has impacted Franklin's social growth with his peer group. The teachers have identified a peer with whom Franklin has a good relationship and who is not easily drawn off task. They obtained permission from both the student and his parents to have that student function as a partner. They established a routine and identified a signal that allows the helper to assist Franklin in identifying when his verbal or motor behavior becomes distracting. The team has role-played scenarios so that the helper knows when to intervene.

Once again, Franklin's collaborative team has recognized the importance of Franklin being in class and benefiting from exposure to regular routines and structures. The teachers have also, however, discussed the need for a more explicit Tier 3 intervention to address the negative habits that Franklin has built up over time. The school behavior specialist has created a plan that provides Franklin with additional behavior intervention time during three thirty-minute sessions throughout the school week. The team has met to decide how to accommodate this while also maintaining the academic focus that will be critical to help Franklin get back on grade before his high school experience begins. Figure 6.13 and figure 6.14 (page 136) are examples of Franklin's completed pro-solve process and subsequent monitoring plan data for Tier 3.

Anna and Heartland High School

To help Anna meet her most significant academic needs, she receives daily support in early literacy and numeracy through a computer-based intervention. A teaching assistant reviews Anna's progress with her in these areas at the conclusion of each week. This Tier 3 intervention supports Anna's significant deficits in critical foundational skills. The goal is to help Anna reach functional levels of literacy and numeracy. School staff provide this intervention in addition to the supports to which Anna has access at Tiers 1 and 2.

In addition to the regular school curriculum, Anna participates in the HHS Avenues program for eleventh-grade students, twelfth-grade students, and those with special

Student: Franklin   **Meeting Date:** October 18

Participants: Mr. Huberman (math teacher), Ms. Fainsilber (ELA/leadership coach), Mr. Springer (counselor), Mrs. Green (principal)

Led by Intervention Team	Targeted Outcomes	1. Concern	2. Cause	3. Desired Outcomes	4. Intervention Steps	5. Who Takes Responsibility
	Foundational reading skills					
	Foundational number sense					
	Foundational writing					
	Foundational language					
	Academic behaviors					
	Social behaviors	Acting out and other off-task behaviors	Distractibility	Set short-term goals for individual tasks and assignments	Three thirty-minute sessions throughout the school week	Mr. Springer
	Health and home					

Next Meeting Date: October 25

Figure 6.13: Franklin's pro-solve Tier 3 targeting process.

Student: Franklin   **Meeting Date:** October 25

Participants: Mr. Huberman (math teacher), Ms. Fainsilber (ELA/leadership coach), Mr. Springer (counselor), Mrs. Green (principal)

	Targeted Outcomes	Desired Outcomes	Interventions and Action Steps	Who	Data Point 1	Data Point 2	Data Point 3	Data Point 4	Data Point 5
Led by Intervention Team	Foundational reading skills								
	Foundational number sense								
	Foundational writing								
	Foundational language								
	Academic behaviors								
	Social behaviors	Set short-term goals for individual tasks and assignments	Three thirty-minute sessions throughout the school week	Mr. Springer	CI/CO goal of self-monitoring (average of 14 daily points/week)	CI/CO goal of self-monitoring (average of 17 daily points/week)	CI/CO goal of self-monitoring (average of 17 daily points/week)		
	Health and home								

Next Meeting Date: November 5

Figure 6.14: Franklin's Pro-solve Tier 3 monitoring plan.

needs. Avenues maintains a focus on maximizing learning for all students at HHS by providing them pathways to pursue their passions. Anna's passion is clearly related to working with animals, and her individual Avenues program is built around preparing her for a future involved with animal care. Because of Anna's impressive functional ability in this area, it is a reasonable postsecondary pathway for her.

On days in which Anna has Avenues classes, she meets with an advisory group consisting of mostly general education students, a regular education teacher, and a special education aide. This advisory group focuses on building strong relationships in a creative, collaborative, and entrepreneurial environment. These staff members then support students as they create projects, set goals, and then work to see their goals come to fruition. The advisory teacher monitors Anna's development in her desired student learning outcomes (DSLOs). These DSLOs include critical thinking, collaboration, communication, creativity and innovation, and character. They are the benchmarks against which all Avenues students are measured and provide clear targets to help guide Anna's learning.

One may think that Anna would be a misfit for the advisory period discussions, but quite the opposite is true. Because Anna thinks differently than other students and is not shy about sharing her views, other students frequently seek out her opinions as her divergent thinking brings new perspectives and ideas to the innovation process for kids. Anna is a valuable part of her advisory.

In Anna's advisory, she interacts with other budding entrepreneurs and has created a business plan associated with a dog-walking service for residents in the neighborhood of the school. Anna's business plan puts the skills she learns in her regular classes to work as she is required to create signs for marketing, manage her profits, and problem solve issues that come up while she walks her clients' dogs. Furthermore, the small amount of money she is paid for her walking services goes in her bank account, something Anna is extremely proud of.

In the Avenues program, Anna splits her time refining her business plan and doing what she loves to do: walking dogs that live in the neighborhood. For now, this is done with guidance, but her goal is to begin to branch out to independent walks in controlled settings. Her progress is documented through a digital portfolio that includes multiple data points. This includes client dog pictures, basic spreadsheets, and documentation of her advertising efforts. Anna's progress toward her educational goals is monitored by her special education teachers who collaborate with Anna's regular education teachers. This collaborative team of educators determines if Anna is meeting her goals by using rubrics that are written in simple language for Anna but align to the same benchmarks of her non–learning-disabled peers.

Though Anna is thriving in this environment, there have been challenges. Anna has made excellent friendships with her like-abled peers but still struggles to connect with students in her elective classes. In addition, though Anna's incontinence has diminished through outside therapy that her parents have arranged, she still struggles with occasional accidents, which are a huge embarrassment for her. Regular meetings with her school counselor to build coping strategies for these emotional setbacks have helped, but the matter is still a constant source of angst for her.

Through a highly collaborative effort, Anna is being challenged to perform at a high level in an environment that prepares her for her future, minimizes her weaknesses, and maximizes her functional strengths in areas of interest to her. Compared to a year ago, Anna is thriving physically, interpersonally, and academically. With the help of a highly structured, creative, and intensive support program, Anna is well on her way to meeting her goals of monitored independent living and fulfilling self-employment. She is currently on track to be one of HHS's first Certificate of Completion students in the area of entrepreneurial business and personal management. Figure 6.15 and figure 6.16 (page 140) are examples of Anna's completed pro-solve process and subsequent monitoring plan data for Tier 3.

Critical Considerations

Creating a master schedule and allocating the resources necessary to make all three tiers of support available to students in need of intensive support can be challenging. Because state requirements, district guidelines, and site resources vary greatly, meeting these outcomes will undoubtedly look different from school to school. While these Tier 3 interventions looked different at the five focus schools in this book, they share some critical considerations in common, including:

Retention Was Not a Viable Option

The research on the effectiveness of retention is abundant and conclusive; retention does not promote higher levels of learning, close achievement gaps, or increase an at-risk student's odds of future success in school. According to arguably the most comprehensive study of what impacts students' learning, *Visible Learning*, author John Hattie (2009) found that being retained one year almost doubled a student's likelihood of dropping out, while being retained twice almost guaranteed it. Hattie states that educators who continue to retain pupils at grade level do so despite cumulative research evidence showing that the potential for negative effects consistently outweighs positive outcomes, and that it would be difficult to find another educational practice for which the evidence is so unequivocally negative. Supporters of retention will say, "But these kids' skills are so low, they can't make it next year." Successful schools can promote students to the next grade *and* provide support in prior skills.

Student: Anna   **Meeting Date:** August 28

Participants: Ms. Meganski (special education teacher), Ms. Bailey (speech pathologist), Ms. Nicholson (special education aide), Mr. Markus (Avenues teacher/advisor), Ms. Lucas (high school counselor), Ms. Gengler (special education teacher), Ms. Mackenzie (school nurse), Mrs. Pearl (principal)

	Targeted Outcomes	1. Concern	2. Cause	3. Desired Outcomes	4. Intervention Steps	5. Who Takes Responsibility
Led by Intervention Team	Foundational reading skills	Reading at a third-grade second-semester level, Anna has shown growth in reading in her past, but it was not sustained due to transience issues	Lacks appropriate skills in comprehension, vocabulary, fluency, and phonetic awareness	To gain one grade level in reading each of her next five years of high school as measured by the Qualitative Reading Inventory (QRI)	One hour additional reading intervention daily with other struggling readers using the DRI reading method Twenty additional minutes daily using Lexia Reading software individually	Ms. Gengler (special education teacher)
	Foundational number sense					
	Foundational writing					
	Foundational language	Underdeveloped expressive language skills are impacting ability to meet life-skills-related goals	Mean length of utterance (MLU) typically registers at five to seven words	MLU of seven to nine words within six months	Meeting with speech pathologist three times per week	Ms. Bailey (speech pathologist)
	Academic behaviors					
	Social behaviors					
	Health and home					

Next Meeting Date: September 15

Figure 6.15: Anna's pro-solve Tier 3 targeting process.

Student: Anna   **Meeting Date:** August 28

Participants: Ms. Meganski (special education teacher), Ms. Bailey (speech pathologist), Ms. Nicholson (special education aide), Mr. Markus (Avenues teacher/advisor), Ms. Lucas (high school counselor), Ms. Gengler (special education teacher), Ms. Mackenzie (school nurse), Mrs. Pearl (principal)

Led by Intervention Team	Targeted Outcomes	Desired Outcomes	Interventions and Action Steps	Who	Data Point 1	Data Point 2	Data Point 3	Data Point 4	Data Point 5
	Foundational reading skills	To gain one grade level in reading each of her next five years of high school as measured by the Qualitative Reading Inventory (QRI)	One hour additional reading intervention daily with other struggling readers using the DRI reading method Twenty additional minutes daily using Lexia Reading software individually	Ms. Gengler (special education teacher)	QRI Oral Reading Rates wpm—62 cwpm—56	QRI Oral Reading Rates wpm—66 cwpm—58	QRI Oral Reading Rates wpm—71 cwpm—63	QRI Oral Reading Rates wpm—74 cwpm—66	QRI Oral Reading Rates wpm—77 cwpm—74
	Foundational number sense								
	Foundational writing								
	Foundational language	MLU of seven to nine words within six months	Meeting with speech pathologist three times per week	Ms. Bailey (speech pathologist)	MLU 5.7	MLU 6.3	MLU 6.4	MLU 6.8	MLU 7.2
	Academic behaviors								
	Social behaviors								
	Health and home								

Next Meeting Date: September 15

Figure 6.16: Anna's pro-solve Tier 3 monitoring plan.

There are rare occasions when a student can be so far behind in remedial skills that he or she cannot derive any benefit from core, grade-level instruction. In these cases, the child may need to receive intensive remedial instruction to build the skills needed to re-enter the core program. An example would be a student brand new to the country who does not have any knowledge of the English language. Given the limitations on time within a school day, the benefits of an intensive English language development program to accelerate the acquisition of conversational English must be weighed against placing this student in grade-level core instruction with the likelihood that access to content may be very limited. But there must be a plan that demonstrates how the child will get caught up and back to grade level. The removal from core instruction must be temporary—just long enough and intensive enough to get the student back into grade-level instruction. If the student never gets back to grade-level curriculum, then the modifications are not an intervention at all, but instead just glorified tracking: expectations are lowered, and the student is tracked into substandard curriculum. This will ensure the student will never catch up and ultimately deny the student any realistic chance to succeed in school and beyond.

The Master Schedule Was Viewed as a Resource to Support Students, Not as an Obstacle to Meeting Student Needs

Throughout our work across North America and beyond, we hear a consistent refrain from far too many schools: "We would like to implement these ideas, but our master schedule just won't allow us." At first glance, this concern is hardly a surprise, as our traditional schedule was never designed to ensure that all students learn at high levels, but instead to create a bell-shaped curve of student results. Yet just because our traditional practices are not aligned to the outcomes described in this book does not mean that we cannot revise our use of school time to achieve these goals.

When we inquire as to why a school states they cannot change their schedule, we are often told that they don't have the authority to make such changes due to state, district, and contractual restraints. Ironically, these same schools change their schedules often throughout the year—for pep rallies, assemblies, fine-arts events, and testing. Similarly, schools do not claim the same restrictions to providing additional enrichment and extension opportunities for gifted, advanced, or extracurricular programs. If a school can create an alternative schedule for a pep rally and advanced programs, then why can't they revise the schedule to create supplemental intervention time and intensive remedial support?

Another common excuse is that there is no time for interventions because there is already too much required curriculum to cover. It is a reality that there is an impossible amount of yearly state curriculum. In fact, there is probably not a teacher in the United States who can honestly say that he or she is able to cover it all within the time constraints of the school year. Subsequently, in individual classrooms, teachers are making time to reteach key concepts by determining what content can be de-emphasized or cut out. If this process can be done by individual teachers, then why can't it be done collectively by a school to create time for interventions? In the end, it is unacceptable to deny struggling students time for interventions due to the desire to keep up the illusion that the school is covering all the required state curriculum.

In reality, the most common reason we see for why most schools don't revise their master schedule is because key adults in the building don't want to change it. Most schools create their master schedule, from teacher assignments to course and subject offerings, based more on the needs and desires of the adults in the building, and less on the needs of the students. Once a school embraces student learning as their mission, a myriad of scheduling options become available. Hundreds and hundreds of schools all over North America have successfully revised their master schedule to achieve the outcomes of core and more and more within existing state guidelines, contractual agreements, and site resources. We have written extensively about some of these schools in our anthology *It's About Time: Planning Interventions and Extensions in Secondary School* (Mattos & Buffum, in press). To identify some of these schools, visit www.allthingsplc.info.

Intensive Interventions Did Not Come at the Cost of Electives and Enrichment

At many schools, providing intensive interventions is viewed as a losing proposition: "To receive remedial help, what must the student lose in his or her current sched-ule?" Most often, we find that the casualty is at-risk students' access to electives and enrichment opportunities. The rationale behind such decisions is that these subjects are nonessential, and repurposing this time is the only way the school can provide intensive support in universal skills. While we agree that students with significant deficits in foundational skills must receive life-altering Tier 3 supports, we would respectfully challenge this thinking, for a number of reasons.

- Enrichment and electives teach universal skills, often through different modalities. If a student is having difficulty in fractions, then learning three-quarters time in music can be an excellent way to teach the concept to students who did not master the skill through repeated abstract whiteboard problems and worksheets. Home economics can teach the same skills as students double a recipe for cookies, while at the same time engaging students in a real-life application of mathematics.

- Enrichment and electives are often seen as the "fun" part of school, subsequently increasing student interest, enthusiasm, and attendance at school. Many schools complain that their most at-risk students are apathetic, while they strip these students from the coursework they enjoy the most, and replace it with a double helping of where they feel the most failure. If teachers were assigned a full schedule of their least favorite teaching assignment, it is likely it would affect their motivation, effort, and attendance, and the adults are getting paid to do it. Why would a child be any different?

While we suspect many schools already acknowledge these benefits, and express an earnest desire to provide all students with intensive support and electives, they will still claim that the schedule just does not allow it. To this claim, we wonder how most schools do not find the same difficulties when scheduling accelerated coursework and electives to their highest-achieving students. For example, a high school might claim that the schedule does not allow for a student at risk to take a grade-level English language arts class (Tier 1) and an intensive reading support class (Tier 3), and keep an elective such as art or drama. Yet it is likely the same school offers advanced placement (AP) courses, in which students take additional academic classes that exceed minimum graduation requirements, and still have access to electives. To extend this example further, if an AP student wanted to take advanced coursework and four years of an elective in foreign language, and was the star quarterback of the football team, and needed to be in physical education with the football team, and was elected ASB president, we bet virtually every high school in America would make the schedule work so that student could participate in all these high-profile opportunities. The student's parents and the community would expect nothing less. If this is the case, then why can't the schedule allow for a student who needs intensive reading help, but loves art, to participate in both? For real-life examples of schools that have achieved these outcomes, visit www.allthingsplc.info.

Resources Were Allotted by Need, Not by Label

If there were no labels in education—regular ed, special ed, Title I, EL, gifted, accelerated—how would a school group students for interventions? Wouldn't it be based on students who have the same needs, such as:

- Students who still struggle with a consonant-vowel-consonant (CVC) blend

- Students who have difficulty multiplying exponents

- Students who are lacking organizational skills to keep track of assignments

And how would a school determine which staff members should lead each of these interventions? Wouldn't it be based on who has training and expertise in teaching CVC blends, algebra, or organizational skills? This thinking makes sense, but is often not the norm, as many schools instead group students by labels tied to funding sources. Such decisions are justified with the claim "But the law does not allow us the flexibility to group students by need." Actually, there is now much more flexibility in federal law and in most state regulations. For example, the federal reauthorization of IDEIA in 2003 promotes early intervening services (EIS), which allow a percentage of special education resources to be used in preventive ways to support students not currently in special education. The example schools in this book moved beyond asking the question, What help does this student qualify for? and instead changed the question to, What does this child need, and who on our staff is best trained to provide this support?

When students have access to potentially all three tiers of support, targeting both skill and will needs, nearly every student should now be on course to achieve the ultimate goal of postsecondary education. Yet there is a likelihood that there still might be a very small handful of students who have not responded to these powerful, proven, research-based interventions. At this point, special education could be an appropriate consideration.

Special Education Identification

We recognize that, despite our best efforts, there will be students who do not respond to high-quality instruction and intervention—at least not yet. Requests for permission to conduct a formal evaluation to determine special education eligibility will still be necessary. This represents one of the most significant moments in a family's life. Educators must make sure it's the right step. The following essential questions (adapted from *Simplifying Response to Intervention*, Buffum et al., 2012, pp. 193–194) ensure that all students have timely access to the time and support they need to learn at high levels. These questions are designed to help an intervention team consider the appropriateness of a referral for a formal evaluation to determine special education eligibility. If the teams cannot answer each question affirmatively, then the decision to recommend special education is not appropriate, justifiable, defendable, or likely to be in a student's best interest.

Essential Questions for Special Education Identification

Tier 1:

- Did the student have access to rigorous, grade-level curriculum?
- Were differentiated practices attempted to ensure that content, process, products, and environments best met the student's needs?
- Were timely small-group supports regularly provided when checks for understanding revealed the need?
- Have scaffolds been put in place so that reading and writing deficits are not responsible for a student's inability to access and demonstrate mastery of grade-level and course essentials?
- Has the student received core support in behavioral, social-emotional, motivational, and attendance areas, and have these factors been considered as possible contributors to difficulties?
- Is there evidence that our school's initial instruction (Tier I) was effective for similar students?

Tier 2:

- Did we identify the student for supplemental time and support in a timely manner?
- Were the specific essential learning targets with which the student had difficulty identified?
- Were alternative strategies, for which there was evidence of effectiveness, used to ensure students mastered the specifically identified essential learning targets?
- Were the causes of the student's inability to master essentials determined?
- Were identified causes addressed through supplemental supports, and were any gaps in immediate prerequisite skills remediated?
- When behavioral, social-emotional, motivational, and attendance areas of concern were present, was reteaching of expectations provided, was the function or purpose of misbehavior determined, were specific behaviors targeted with specific evidence-based strategies, did all related staff receive professional development in the procedures, and was progress monitored and adjusted through a mentoring process, such as CI/CO?
- Were research-based and evidence-based interventions used to target the student's specific learning needs?
- Is there evidence that our school's supplemental intervention (Tier 2) was effective for similar students?

Tier 3:

- Was the student screened or identified to have significant deficits in foundational prerequisite skills in a timely manner?
- Were the specific causes of significant deficits analyzed and specific skill targets determined?
- Were intensive, targeted (Tier 3) interventions provided as a result of these analyses?
- When behavioral, social-emotional, motivational, and attendance areas of concern were present, were more formal functional behavioral analyses completed, were

Continued →

specific behavior intervention plans developed that targeted specific behaviors with specific evidence-based strategies, was progress monitored and mentored, and did all related staff receive professional development in the procedures?

- Were members of the intervention team (clinicians, speech and language pathologists, occupational therapists, special education staff, librarians, nurses) involved in a problem-solving process so that different experiences, perspectives, and expertise could be leveraged to identify the student's specific learning needs and the causes of his or her struggles?

- Were research-based interventions used to address the student's specific learning needs?

- Is there evidence that our school's intensive interventions (Tier 3) were effective for similar students?

- Are there any other interventions or supports that can or should be tried before considering special education placement?

- Have the teams brainstormed the supports that could be provided if the student is determined eligible for special education that cannot be provided now?

- Have teams identified the progress that will be needed and the conditions that will need to exist for the student to ultimately exit special education?

- Do we have agreement among the intervention team that special education is necessary and appropriate to meet the needs of this child? Is this decision defensible?

We must ensure that all students gain access to core content that will enable them to live productive lives. We can predict that despite our best, first instruction, some students will need more time and alternative interventions to help them reach mastery of the essentials of core content. We can further predict that some students will need intensive supports to address significant deficits in foundational skills. Teams must plan for solutions at Tiers 1, 2, and 3 to meet the varied needs of all students within their schools.

CHAPTER 7

Getting Started and Getting Better

What if a school committed to intervening as early as possible for students experiencing difficulty in learning and behaving, to proactively supporting students in a timely manner with targeted supports, and to building such commitments into the very fabric of the school and the way educators go about their daily business?

RTI at Work represents our concerted, collective, coordinated efforts to systematize support for all students. With RTI at Work, in correlation with the PLC at Work™ process and PBIS, educators structure their collaborative time and school schedules to ensure that all students receive the time and support needed to learn at high levels—to graduate ready for college or a skilled career.

The Five Students and the Four Cs

As we conclude this book, we want to revisit our five students and reflect on how interventions and instructional approaches have worked for them. A quick review of each student, his or her needs at each tier, and the plans that were enacted will connect us back to the goal identified at the beginning of this book: that we view our efforts on behalf of students needing academic and behavior interventions as an opportunity for discovery rather than as a dilemma.

Armando and Robinson Elementary

Armando is our first-grade student who exhibited immaturity and had deficits in social skills. His reading success when presented with words on a page allowed for his phonics skills to progress at a greater rate than his phonological skills, but his inattentiveness seemed to compromise his skills at making meaning of text when reading independently or without oral supports. Armando's overall difficulties with fine motor skills inhibited his writing. His inability to make close friends was driven by his difficulties in following rules, which frustrated his peers who grew weary of his disruptions. The teachers on his team realized that their Tier 1 core supports were not enough in the areas of reading and social behaviors, although they were more than adequate for the majority of the students. Their Tier 2 interventions involved more time and an alternative approach to mastering essential standards. Additionally, Armando required more frequent and specific supports with respect, responsibility, and readiness. At Tier 3, staff addressed his significant deficits in the foundational skill of phonics and provided time for a computer-based intervention that exercised his memory and attention while improving his abilities at processing and sequencing. Armando has responded positively to the specific, individualized interventions, and the classroom has become a more positive environment for all learners.

Katie and Wilson Elementary

Katie is our fourth-grade student who was well behaved, compliant, and shy. Periodically, she had difficulty comprehending texts she read, either independently or with the rest of the class. Her fluency rate was low but within the normal range. She made regular errors when she encountered multisyllabic words. While Katie's writing contained a few conventional errors, she wrote and drew voluminously. The larger areas of concern for Katie were social-emotional. Katie's social-emotional needs were a concern as she was reluctant to allow herself to get close to any staff member. The team made it a priority to establish a meaningful connection with Katie, with one team member taking the responsibility to connect with her every day. Katie's team recognized that her social-emotional needs were increasingly impacting her academic performance and mental health, and Tier 3 supports were initiated. Staff have seen progress through the initiation of intensive support and will continue with that approach while also engaging one of the key interventionists from the school to continue the progress in this critical area.

Holly and Roosevelt Elementary

Holly is our sixth-grade student who had been receiving supports in her school district since she was three years of age. She was diagnosed with severe autism just before her third birthday and is effectively mute. Holly experiences behavioral challenges in the areas of socially appropriate actions and visual-perceptual and sensory-processing domains. At Tier 1, her team tailored an instructional program to build Holly's literacy and numeracy skills. At Tier 2, Holly's core curriculum included explicit instruction in sign language and focused on her ability to read (or sign) words by sight. At Tier 3, Holly participated in a group with students from fourth, fifth, and sixth grade, all of whom have reading levels in the second- to third-grade range. The end result has been an increase in positive social interactions for Holly and an opportunity for growth as a leader sharing her proficiency in American Sign Language.

Franklin and Middletown Middle School

Franklin is our academically gifted student who was often bored with school and rarely challenged by academic expectations. He thrived on being the class clown while struggling with organizational skills as related to work completion. His relative ease in elementary school had him feeling that he learned more on his own than in the structured environment of school. His lack of focus on the tasks at hand resulted in low achievement. At Tier 1, the goal was to lessen Franklin's distractibility, which his team recognized as an antecedent to more serious negative behavior. They quickly realized that Tier 2 intervention was required as Franklin's behavior over time led to him missing instruction, resulting in a lack of proficiency in the skills that would allow him to complete tasks in a timely fashion. His Tier 3 challenges stemmed from these ongoing struggles, and the team addressed his frequent disruptions in class, his calling out, his daydreaming, and his being easily distracted. By challenging him academically and focusing his energy on task completion, the team feels it is making inroads and setting Franklin up positively for his transition to high school.

Anna and Heartland High School

Anna is our upbeat and outgoing tenth-grade student who had attended five different schools growing up. Her multiple cognitive and physical disabilities hampered her ability to access the typical school curriculum, and she had trouble connecting with her grade-level peers. Her physical handicaps were present at birth and resulted in eligibility for an IEP. At Tier 1, Anna's academic program was significantly modified to meet her struggles with basic numerical functions, her developing knowledge of phonics, and her weak fluency and comprehension skills. At Tier 2, Anna had access to more time and differentiated supports to master the essential learning that the school teams established. At Tier 3, Anna received daily support in early literacy and numeracy through a computer-based intervention, which supported her significant deficits in critical foundational skills. As Anna grew in confidence, her natural strengths in socializing allowed her to make connections with other students and build supports that further aided her academic growth.

Taking Responsibility for All Learners

Throughout this book, we have emphasized embracing the "genius of the AND" and avoiding the "tyranny of the OR" (Collins & Porras, 2004), which often requires stretching beyond what is comfortable and convenient as educators work in concert with students to maximize student outcomes. Chapter 3 highlighted this process of successfully responding when students need additional support by avoiding the often-used approach of deciding that struggles require either schoolwide protocols designed to classify student needs into predetermined interventions *or* a problem-solving process designed to dig deeply into the individual needs of each student needing extra help. The pro-solve process utilizes protocol-driven *and* problem-solving processes. Protocols create an effective, systematic process while problem solving enables a school to tailor its collective efforts to the unique needs of each student. In terms of our five students, this structure has provided the steps to identify each student's academic and behavioral needs, determine interventions, and establish specific staff responsibilities to successfully implement and monitor the plan.

The Four Cs

The four *Cs*—collective responsibility, concentrated instruction, convergent assessment, and certain access—are the filters through which teams make the instructional decisions to generate the best possible outcomes for students. Our school teams identified the talents each team member had and could bring to the needs identified for each student.

By focusing their instruction and frequently assessing to measure progress toward desired outcomes, they effectively measured their individual and collective impact. This ensured that all students had access to the interventions they needed in a timely fashion. Ultimately, we return to the premise of the opening chapter as educators shift from traditional, reactive intervention practices that focus on labeling the challenges of struggling students as either skill or will problems to a tiered, proactive process that serves the whole child, providing whatever supports are needed so students can learn at the highest levels of their unique talents and abilities.

Schools and teams must ensure that their practices align with the four essential guiding principles of RTI at Work.

Collective Responsibility

Staffs must have honest conversations about their beliefs in all students learning at high levels. They must be willing to make collective commitments to the practices and actions that explicitly demonstrate these beliefs. They must trust one another and believe in their own, and their colleagues', capacities for making certain that college and career readiness is a constant. All staff members' words and actions support the following ideas.

- Every student can learn. Any student who will be expected to live an independent adult life must be expected to master the essentials of a grade or course.

- All staff take responsibility for all students.

- Staff make decisions based on evidence and research, not based on past practices, preferences, or opinions.

- Staff focus on what we can control.

- Staff hold one another accountable.

Individual staff members make personal commitments, and teams of staff members make collective commitments. Staff members do not focus on what students need to do, what parents need to do, or what other teams need to do, unless they are prepared to actively partner with these stakeholders in the continuous-improvement process.

A commitment to collective responsibility necessitates that teams have clearly defined roles and responsibilities, that team efforts are coordinated, and that important information is efficiently communicated and used to inform future practices.

Concentrated Instruction and Convergent Assessment

Without a collaboratively defined focus and clarity regarding desired outcomes for which all students will demonstrate mastery, we will continue to be plagued by a curriculum that is a mile wide and an inch deep. Breadth will continue to be the enemy of depth of understanding. Retention of knowledge and the ability to apply learning will suffer as a result of attempting to cover too much. We will continue to leave students behind, fail to engage students in relevant learning opportunities, and misdiagnose students with learning disabilities who are, in fact, casualties of an unfocused curriculum. Problem solving and critical thinking must be prioritized outcomes for students, and we must plan the time for these outcomes to be met.

We must also collaboratively create measures of our effectiveness and of student learning. Common assessments are the key levers of RTI, representing the mastery for which we will prepare students and providing the evidence of necessary next steps. Assessments, collaboratively created, administered, and analyzed, provide evidence that allows teams to collectively respond, thereby converging our knowledge of our effectiveness and of students' needs. We must ask:

- Are our academic and behavioral outcomes clearly defined and prioritized so that they represent a viable quantity of content that all students can master?

- Do we have common (but flexible) pacing guides:
  - So that we can collaboratively plan?
  - And commonly assess?
  - And collectively respond?
- Do we commonly and frequently gather evidence to inform:
  - How well we have done ensuring that students master essentials?
  - Which students require more time and different approaches?
  - With which essential content do students require more time and different approaches?

Instruction and assessment, concentrated and convergent, must increasingly represent mutually reinforcing practices by schools and teams. Collaboratively defined and prioritized outcomes provide the content that we will measure with assessments, commonly created assessments help focus our instruction and instructional practices, and evidence from assessments informs adjustments to future instruction and intervention.

Certain Access

Schools have a golden opportunity to provide proactive supports for students most at risk. We must take advantage of this opportunity more consistently and with a greater sense of urgency.

We can identify students prior to the beginning of any school year who will experience difficulties and will be at grave risk for failure and frustration. These students have significant deficits in the foundational skills of reading, writing, numeracy, English language, attendance, or behavior. Collectively, we know who these students are or, without a laborious process, could identify these students. This process is known as universal screening, and when proactively led by our schoolwide teams, the process can ensure that intensive and targeted Tier 3 supports are provided in a timely manner for students most at risk.

Universal screening measures address the following key questions.

- What criteria will we use to determine if a student is in need of intensive support?
- What screening assessment or process will we use to identify students in need of intensive support?
- When will the screening process take place?

- Who will administer the screening?
- What intensive interventions will we use to accelerate student learning and support the identified students?

As a school, we know that all students must graduate with the skills that will prepare them to enter college or a skilled career if they are to have a chance at a middle-class life, so we have committed to high levels of learning for all students. We know that students with significant deficits in foundational skills are at risk of missing out on this opportunity and at risk of immediate failure and frustration in the absence of intensive, lifesaving supports. We can know who these students are at our schools, so we can determine their needs and provide targeted interventions. We know, or can know; we must do. We must close the knowing-doing gap, proactively screening students who are at risk before the year even begins so that we can provide timely and intensive Tier 3 supports.

While we wrote this book from the perspective of how individual students can benefit from a school that takes collective responsibility for student learning and provides multiple tiers of timely, systematic support to ensure this outcome, we would argue that such a system would be equally beneficial to the noble educators who have dedicated their lives to the service of our children. Our current system asks individual teachers to do what is virtually impossible—to have a single teacher meet the skill and will needs of every student assigned to his or her classroom. Educators work tirelessly to achieve this goal, but most quit within five years of entering the profession, having given it their all and realizing that some students still fail. When a school creates a collective system of interventions, like the examples provided in this book, then help would be available for not only every student, but also for every educator in the building.

Let us end our journey together by looking at the work ahead from one last perspective. Imagine for a moment that one of our five fictional students—Armando, Katie, Holly, Franklin, or Anna—was a member of your family, your own son or daughter, niece or nephew, brother or sister, cousin, or grandchild. What kind of school would you want this student to attend? Wouldn't you want his or her schools to be like the ones described throughout this book—schools in which the staff assume every child can learn at high levels, see both the strengths and needs in every student, and then work collaboratively to meet these needs? If this is what we would want for our own child, then every student deserves nothing less.

References and Resources

ACT. (2006). *Ready for college and ready for work: Same or different?* Iowa City, IA: Author.

Ainsworth, L. (2003a). *Power standards: Identifying the standards that matter the most.* Denver, CO: Advanced Learning Press.

Ainsworth, L. (2003b). *"Unwrapping" the standards: A simple process to make standards manageable.* Denver, CO: Advanced Learning Press.

Ainsworth, L., & Viegut, D. (2006). *Common formative assessments: How to connect standards-based instruction and assessment.* Thousand Oaks, CA: Corwin Press.

Bender, W. N. (2009). *Beyond the RTI pyramid: Solutions for the first years of implementation.* Bloomington, IN: Solution Tree Press.

Bender, W. N. (2012). *RTI in middle and high schools.* Bloomington, IN: Solution Tree Press.

Berger, J., & Parkin, A. (2006). *The value of a degree: Education, employment, and earnings in Canada.* Accessed at www.chs.ca/sites/default/files/uploads/value_of_education_with_degree.pdf on April 7, 2014.

Bloom, B. S. (1968). Learning for mastery. *Evaluation Comment, 1*(2), 1–12.

Bloom, B. S., Engelhart, M. D., Furst, E. J., Hill, W. H., & Krathwohl, D. R. (1956). *Taxonomy of educational objectives: The classification of educational goals—Handbook I, cognitive domain.* New York: Longman.

Brantlinger, E. A. (Ed.). (2006). *Who benefits from special education?: Remediating (fixing) other people's children.* Mahwah, NJ: Erlbaum.

The Bridge School. (2005). *Archives: Meeting Dr. Stephen Hawking.* Accessed at http://archive.today /xbUbt on September 25, 2014.

Buffum, A., Mattos, M., & Weber, C. (2009). *Pyramid response to intervention: RTI, professional learning communities, and how to respond when kids don't learn.* Bloomington, IN: Solution Tree Press.

Buffum, A., Mattos, M., & Weber, C. (2010). The why behind RTI. *Educational Leadership, 68*(2), 10–16.

Buffum, A., Mattos, M., & Weber, C. (2012). *Simplifying response to intervention: Four essential guiding principles.* Bloomington, IN: Solution Tree Press.

Bureau of Labor Statistics. (2013). *Education and training outlook for occupations, 2011–22*. Washington, DC: U.S. Department of Labor. Accessed at www.bls.gov/emp/ep_edtrain_outlook.pdf on April 7, 2014.

Chao, E. L. (2008, June 23). *Remarks prepared for delivery by U.S. Secretary of Labor Elaine L. Chao to the Greater Louisville Inc. Metro Chamber of Commerce*. Washington, DC: U.S. Department of Labor. Accessed at www.dol.gov/_sec/media/speeches/20080623_COC.htm on April 7, 2014.

Chicken or the egg. (n.d.). In *Wikipedia*. Accessed at http://en.wikipedia.org/wiki/Chicken_or_the_egg on August 6, 2014.

Collins, J. (2005). Good to Great *and the social sectors: A monograph to accompany* Good to Great. New York: HarperCollins.

Collins, J., & Porras, J. I. (2004). *Built to last: Successful habits of visionary companies*. New York: HarperCollins.

Conley, D. T. (2007). *Redefining college readiness*. Eugene, OR: Educational Policy Improvement Center.

Cooper, D. (2011). *Redefining fair: How to plan, assess, and grade for excellence in mixed-ability classrooms*. Bloomington, IN: Solution Tree Press.

Dolan, R. P., & Hall, T. E. (2001). Universal design for learning: Implications for large-scale assessment. *IDA Perspectives, 27*(4), 22–25.

Donovan, M. S., & Cross, C. T. (Eds.). (2002). *Minority students in special and gifted education*. Washington, DC: National Academies Press.

DuFour, R., DuFour, R., Eaker, R., & Many, T. (2006). *Learning by doing: A handbook for Professional Learning Communities at Work*™. Bloomington, IN: Solution Tree Press.

DuFour, R., DuFour, R., Eaker, R., & Many, T. (2010). *Learning by doing: A handbook for Professional Learning Communities at Work*™ (2nd ed.). Bloomington, IN: Solution Tree Press.

Elmore, R. (1996). Getting to scale with good. *Harvard Educational Review, 66*(1), 1–26.

Fénelon, F. (1825). *Lives of the ancient philosophers*. (Original work published 1726).

Ferri, B. A., & Connor, D. J. (2006). *Reading resistance: Discourses of exclusion in desegregation and inclusion debates*. New York: Peter Lang.

Fleming, C. B., Harachi, T. W., Cortes, R. C., Abbott, R. D., & Catalano, R. F. (2004). Level and change in reading scores and attention problems during elementary school as predictors of problem behavior in middle school. *Journal of Emotional and Behavioral Disorders, 12*(3), 130–144.

Fletcher, J. M., & Vaughn, S. (2009). RTI models as alternatives to traditional views of learning disabilities: Response to the commentaries. *Child Development Perspectives, 3*(1), 48–50.

Friedman, T. L. (2005). *The world is flat: A brief history of the twenty-first century*. New York: Farrar, Straus and Giroux.

Fuchs, L. S., & Fuchs, D. (2007). A model for implementing responsiveness to intervention. *Teaching Exceptional Children, 39*(5), 14–20.

Goldin, C., & Katz, L. F. (2007). *The race between education and technology: The evolution of U.S. educational wage differentials, 1890 to 2005*. Cambridge, MA: National Bureau of Economic Research.

Gunderson, S. (2013, September 27). The postsecondary education investment [Web log post]. Accessed at http://blogs.reuters.com/great-debate/2013/09/27/the-postsecondary-education-investment on April 7, 2014.

Guskey, T. R. (2003). How classroom assessments can improve learning. *Educational Leadership, 60*(5), 6–11.

Hattie, J. (2009). *Visible learning: A synthesis of over 800 meta-analyses relating to achievement*. New York: Routledge.

Hays, S. (1994). Structure and agency and the sticky problem of culture. *Sociological Theory, 12*(1), 57–72. Accessed at http://links.jstor.org/sici?sici=0735-2751%28199403%2912%3A1%3C57%3ASAAATS%3E2.0.CO%3B2-J on September 25, 2014.

Hierck, T., Coleman, C., & Weber, C. (2011). *Pyramid of behavior interventions: Seven keys to a positive learning environment*. Bloomington, IN: Solution Tree Press.

Jerald, C. D. (2009). *Defining a 21st century education*. Alexandria, VA: Center for Public Education.

Karoly, L. A., & Panis, C. W. A. (2004). *The 21st century at work: Forces shaping the future workforce and workplace in the United States*. Santa Monica, CA: RAND.

Langan, C. M. (2001). *Which came first . . .* Accessed at www.megafoundation.org/CTMU/Articles/Which.html on August 2, 2008.

Marzano, R. J. (2003). *What works in schools: Translating research into action*. Alexandria, VA: Association for Supervision and Curriculum Development.

Mattos, M., & Buffum, A. (in press). *It's about time: Planning interventions and extensions in secondary school*. Bloomington, IN: Solution Tree Press.

McGraw-Hill Education. (2009, October 29). *McGraw-Hill Education underscores commitment to teaching struggling students*. Accessed at www.rand.org/health/projects/cbits.html on September 25, 2014.

McLaughlin, M. W., & Talbert, J. E. (2006). *Building school-based teacher learning communities: Professional strategies to improve student achievement*. New York: Teachers College Press.

Morrison, G. M., Anthony, S., Storino, M., & Dillon, C. (2001). An examination of the disciplinary histories and the individual and educational characteristics of students who participate in an in-school suspension program. *Education and Treatment of Children, 24*(3), 276–293.

Mortenson, T. (2007). Average family income by educational attainment of householder 1967 to 2006. *Postsecondary Education Opportunity, 185*, 14–16.

Mullis, I. V. S., Martin, M. O., Olson, J. F., Berger, D. R., Milne, D., & Stanco, G. M. (Eds.). (2008). *TIMSS 2007 encyclopedia: A guide to mathematics and science education around the world* (Vols. 1 and 2). Chestnut Hill, MA: TIMSS and PIRLS International Study Center.

Nelson, J. R., Benner, G. J., Lane, K., & Smith, B. W. (2004). Academic achievement of K–12 students with emotional and behavioral disorders. *Exceptional Children, 71*(1), 59–73.

O'Toole, J., & Lawler, E. E., III. (2006). *The new American workplace*. New York: Palgrave Macmillan.

RAND Corporation. (2013). *Cognitive-behavioral intervention for trauma in schools*.

Reeves, D. B. (2002). *Making standards work: How to implement standards-based assessments in the classroom, school, and district* (3rd ed.). Denver, CO: Advanced Learning Press.

Ritchey, K. D., & Goeke, J. L. (2006). Orton-Gillingham and Orton-Gillingham–based reading instruction: A review of the literature. *Journal of Special Education, 40*(3), 171–183.

Scherer, M. (2001). How and why standards can improve student achievement: A conversation with Robert J. Marzano. *Educational Leadership, 59*(1), 14–18.

Senge, P. M. (1990). *The fifth discipline: The art and practice of the learning organization*. New York: Doubleday.

Simonsen, B., Sugai, G., & Negron, M. (2008). Schoolwide positive behavior supports: Primary systems and practices. *Teaching Exceptional Children, 40*(6), 32–40.

Skiba, R. J., Poloni-Staudinger, L., Gallini, S., Simmons, A. B., & Feggins-Azziz, R. (2006). Disparate access: The disproportionality of African American students with disabilities across educational environments. *Exceptional Children, 72*(4), 411–424.

Skiba, R. J., Simmons, A. B., Ritter, S., Gibb, A. C., Rausch, M. K., Cuadrado, J., et al. (2008). Achieving equity in special education: History, status, and current challenges. *Exceptional Children, 74*(3), 264–288.

Smith, P., & Daniel, C. (2000). *The chicken book*. Athens, GA: University of Georgia Press.

Stiggins, R. (2004). New assessment beliefs for a new school mission. *Phi Delta Kappan, 86*(1), 22–27.

Sugai, G. (2001, June 23). *School climate and discipline: Schoolwide positive behavior support*. Keynote presentation to and paper for the National Summit on the Shared Implementation of IDEA, Washington, DC.

Sugai, G., & Horner, R. (2002). The evolution of discipline practices: School-wide positive behavior supports. *Child & Family Behavior Therapy, 24*(1–2), 23–50.

Waller, J. (1998). *Face to face: The changing state of racism across America*. New York: Basic Books.

Weiner, C. (2013, October 10). Earnings gap narrows between recent college and high school graduates. *The Daily Californian*. Accessed at www.dailycal.org/2013/10/10/earnings-gap-narrows-recent-college -high-school-graduates on October 10, 2013.

Wiggins, G., & McTighe, J. (2005). *Understanding by design* (expanded 2nd ed.). Alexandria, VA: Association for Supervision and Curriculum Development.

Wiliam, D. (2011). *Embedded formative assessment*. Bloomington, IN: Solution Tree Press.

Index

A

academic behaviors, 6
  addressing, 80–82
academic skills and knowledge, 5–6
ACT, 3
Ainsworth, L., 23, 24, 25
Anna and Heartland High School
  background information, 39–41
  four Cs and summary, 149
  instruction and interventions, uniting, 75
  instruction and remediation, uniting, 134,
    137–138, 139–140
  skill and supplemental interventions, uniting,
    97, 100–105
Aristotle, 1
Armando and Robinson Elementary
  background information, 30–32
  four Cs and summary, 147–148
  instruction and interventions, uniting, 69–72
  instruction and remediation, uniting, 123–
    125, 126–127
  skill and supplemental interventions, uniting,
    84–88
assumptions, adopting fundamental, 61–62

B

behavioral RTI, 26
behavioral strategies, employing, 82
behavior and attendance progress monitoring,
  55–59
behavior document form, 66, 67

behavior intervention plan (BIP), 122
Bender, W., 26
Bloom, B., 23
Bloom's taxonomy, 5
Buffum, A., 11, 12–13, 14, 21, 114, 121, 142

C

certain access, 13, 25–27, 68, 152–153
check-in/check-out (CI/CO), 55–56, 57, 82,
  83–84, 123
Cognitive Behavioral Intervention for Trauma
  in Schools, 128
Coleman, C., 11, 65, 121
collaborative culture, 21
collaborative teacher teams, 18
  responsibilities, 51, 109, 111
collective responsibility, 12, 21–22, 61–62,
  150–151
Collins, J., 12
common assessment team protocol, 79–80
Common Core State Standards (CCSS), 6
common formative assessments (CFAs), 66
  analyzing, 78–80
  crafting, 78
  responding to, 80
Common Formative Assessments (Ainsworth and
  Viegut), 25
concentrated instruction, 12, 23–24, 62–66,
  151–152
Conley, D., 5–6
content knowledge, 5
convergent assessment, 12, 24–25, 151–152

Cooper, D., 25
culture, use of term, 61
curriculum-based measurements (CBMs), 83,
    117, 121, 122–123

D
Darwin, C., 1
Defining a 21st Century Education (Jerald), 3
DuFour, R., 7–8

E
Eaker, R., 7–8
early intervention services (EIS), 144
education
    future needs and, 2–3
    lifelong learning, 3–4
    organization/employment structure changes
        and impact on, 4–7
    purpose of, 2
electives, need to incorporate, 142–143
Elmore, R., 17
Embedded Formative Assessment (Wiliam), 25
essential standards, unwrapping, 78
Essential Standards Chart, 63, 64
expectations, common, 65

F
fidelity to standards, 63
Fifth Discipline, The (Senge), 21–22
Fletcher, J., 26
focus on learning, 21
foundational skills, 5
four Cs of RTI at Work
    certain access, 13, 25–27, 68, 152–153
    collective responsibility, 12, 21–22, 61–62,
        150–151
    concentrated instruction, 12, 23–24, 62–66,
        151–152
    convergent assessment, 12, 24–25, 151–152
framework, defined, 17
Franklin and Middletown Middle School
    background information, 37–38
    four Cs and summary, 149
    instruction and interventions, uniting, 74–75
    instruction and remediation, uniting, 131,
        134, 135–136
    skill and supplemental interventions, uniting,
        93, 96–97, 98–99
Friedman, T., 4

Fuchs, D., 26
Fuchs, L., 26
functional behavioral analysis (FBA), 55,
    121–122

G
Goldin, C., 3
Good to Great (Collins), 12
Guskey, T., 25

H
Hattie, J., 26, 62, 138
Hawking, S., 1
Hays, K., 17
Hierck, T., 11, 65, 121
higher-level thinking, 5–6
Holly and Roosevelt Elementary
    background information, 35–37
    four Cs and summary, 148–149
    instruction and interventions, uniting, 73–74
    instruction and remediation, uniting, 128,
        131, 132–133
    skill and supplemental interventions, uniting,
        90, 93, 94–95
Horner, R., 9, 26

I
IDEIA, 144
instruction
    concentrated, 12, 23–24, 62–66, 151–152
    targeted, 65
interventions
    identifying students for intensive, 112,
        114–116
    targeting, 77–80
intervention teams, schoolwide. *See* schoolwide
    intervention teams
*It's About Time: Planning Interventions and
    Extensions* (Buffum and Mattos), 142

J
Jerald, C. D., 3, 5

K
Karoly, L. A., 3–4
Katie and Wilson Elementary
    background information, 32–34
    four Cs and summary, 148
    instruction and interventions, uniting, 72–73

instruction and remediation, uniting, 125, 128, 129–130

skill and supplemental interventions, uniting, 89–90, 91–92

Katz, L., 3

L

Lawler, E., 4

leadership teams, schoolwide. *See* schoolwide leadership teams

learning, lifelong, 3–4

M

Macrobius, 1

Making Standards Work (Reeves), 23

Marzano, R., 23

mastery learning, 23

Mattos, M., 11, 12–13, 14, 21, 114, 121, 142

McLaughlin, M., 21

McTighe, J., 23

N

New American Workplace, The (O'Toole and Lawler), 4

O

organization structure, changes to, 4–7

O'Toole, J., 4

P

Panis, C.W.A., 3–4

positive behavior interventions and supports (PBIS), 26

power standards, 24

Power Standards (Ainsworth), 23

problem-solving process, 44–46

professional learning communities (PLCs), 7–8, 10, 11

progress monitoring

behavior and attendance, 55–59

role of, 54–55, 82–84

Tier 2, 55, 56

Tier 3, 117, 120

tools, types of, 59

Pro-Solve Intervention Targeting Protocol

description of, 44–46

Tier 1 and Tier 2 and, 49, 51, 52–53

Tier 3 and, 116–123

pyramid approach, integrated, 11

Pyramid of Behavior Interventions: Seven Keys to a Positive Learning Environment (Hierck, Coleman, and Weber), 11, 65, 121

Pyramid Response to Intervention: RTI, Professional Learning Communities, and How to Respond When Kids Don't Learn (Buffum, Mattos, and Weber), 11

R

RAND, 3

Redefining Fair (Cooper), 25

Reeves, D., 23, 24, 63

reinforcement, positive, 65–66

resources, student needs and, 143–144

response to intervention (RTI), 8–9, 10, 11

Response to Intervention at Work pyramid, 13–14

See also four Cs of RTI at Work; Pro-Solve Intervention Targeting Protocol

inverted pyramid, 46–47

misapplications of, 46–49

outcomes and interventions, 49, 50, 110

responsibility and collaboration, need for individual, 4–7

retention, problem with, 138, 141

S

scheduling, problem with master, 141–142

School-Wide Information System (SWIS), 66

schoolwide intervention teams, 20

responsibilities of, 111–112, 113

schoolwide leadership teams, 18–20

responsibilities of, 51, 54, 109, 111, 112

schoolwide positive behavior supports (SWPBS), 9–10, 11

screening, universal, 112, 114–116

SDAIE (specially designed academic instruction in English), 71

Senge, P., 21–22

Simplified Functional Behavioral Analysis, 81

Simplifying Response to Intervention: Four Essential Guiding Principles (Buffum, Mattos, and Weber), 12–13, 14, 114, 121

skill-or-will dilemma, 2, 12

skills, universal, 107–108

social behaviors, 6–7

addressing, 80–82

special education identification, 144–146

standards

prioritizing, 62–66
unwrapping essential, 78
Stiggins, R., 25
student learning, factors that impact, 62
students and schools, description of
   Anna and Heartland High School, 39–41,
      75, 97, 100–105, 134, 137–138, 139–
      140, 149
   Armando and Robinson Elementary, 30–32,
      69–72, 84–88, 123–125, 126–127,
      147–148
   characteristics of, 29
   Franklin and Middletown Middle School,
      37–38, 74–75, 93, 96–97, 98–99, 131,
      134, 135–136, 149
   Holly and Roosevelt Elementary, 35–37,
      73–74, 90, 93, 94–95, 128, 131, 132–
      133, 148–149
   Katie and Wilson Elementary, 32–34, 72–73,
      89–90, 91–92, 125, 128, 129–130, 148
Sugai, G., 9, 11, 26

T

Talbert, J., 21
Teaching-Assessing Cycle, 81
teams
   collaborative teacher, 18, 51, 109, 111
   schoolwide intervention, 20, 111–112, 113
   schoolwide leadership, 18–20, 51, 54, 109,
      111, 112
Tier 1, Pro-Solve Intervention Targeting
      Protocol and, 49, 51, 52–53
Tier 2
   progress monitoring, 55, 56
   Pro-Solve Intervention Targeting Protocol
      and, 49, 51, 52–53
Tier 3
   critical considerations, 138, 141–144
   progress monitoring, 117, 120
   Pro-Solve Intervention Targeting Protocol
      and, 116–123
*21st Century at Work: Forces Shaping the Future
      Workforce and Workplace in the United
      States, The* (Karoly and Panis, 3–4

U

Understanding by Design (Wiggins and
      McTighe), 23
Universal Design for Learning, 26
universal screening, 112, 114–116
Universal Screening Planning Guide, 114–116
unwrapping essential standards, 78
"Unwrapping" the Standards (Ainsworth), 23

V

Vaughn, S., 26
Viegut, D., 25
Visible Learning (Hattie), 26, 62, 138

W

Weber, C., 11, 12–13, 14, 21, 65, 114, 121
Wiggins, G., 23
Wiliam, D., 25
World Is Flat, The (Friedman), 4

Pyramid of Behavior Interventions
Tom Hierck, Charlie Coleman, and Chris Weber
Students thrive when educators commit to proactively meeting their behavioral as well as academic needs. This book will help teachers and school leaders transform the research on behavior, response to intervention, and professional learning communities into practical strategies they can use to create a school culture and classroom climates in which learning is primed to occur.
BKF532

Using Formative Assessment in the RTI Framework
Kay Burke and Eileen Depka
RTI and formative assessment have the potential to positively impact student achievement. Understand the basics of RTI and its connection to formative assessment, and base instructional decisions on the results of effective formative assessment practices. Learn how to adjust instruction to increase levels of student understanding and achievement with the information, tools, and techniques presented in this practical guide.
BKF369

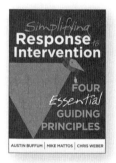

Simplifying Response to Intervention
Austin Buffum, Mike Mattos, and Chris Weber
The sequel to *Pyramid Response to Intervention* advocates that a successful RTI model begins by asking the right questions to create a fundamentally effective learning environment for every student. RTI is not a series of implementation steps, but rather a way of thinking. Understand why bureaucratic, paperwork-heavy, compliance-oriented, test-score-driven approaches fail. Then learn how to create a focused RTI model that works.
BKF506

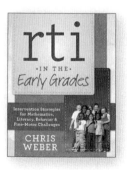

RTI in the Early Grades
Chris Weber
Explore why intervention and support for struggling students in the early grades are essential to student success. Teachers and support personnel will discover how to implement RTI-based supports in the early grades and learn what this prevention looks like. Find practical, research-based strategies to seal the gaps in student learning in grades K–3, identify students who need intervention, and more.
BKF572

Solution Tree | Press
a division of
Solution Tree

Visit solution-tree.com or call 800.733.6786 to order.

Wait! Your professional development journey doesn't have to end with the last pages of this book.

We realize improving student learning doesn't happen overnight. And your school or district shouldn't be left to puzzle out all the details of this process alone.

No matter where you are on the journey, we're committed to helping you get to the next stage.

Take advantage of everything from **custom workshops** to **keynote presentations** and **interactive web and video conferencing**. We can even help you develop an action plan tailored to fit your specific needs.

Let's get the conversation started.

Call 888.763.9045 today.

solution-tree.com